A WOMAN TENDERFOOT

GRACE GALLATIN SETON-THOMPSON

1st WORLD
LIBRARY
Literary Society

A Woman Tenderfoot

Grace Gallatin Seton-Thompson

© 1st World Library – Literary Society, 2005
PO Box 2211
Fairfield, IA 52556
www.1stworldlibrary.org
First Edition

LCCN: 2004195626

Softcover ISBN: 1-4218-0447-6
Hardcover ISBN: 1-4218-0347-X
eBook ISBN: 1-4218-0547-2

Purchase *"A Woman Tenderfoot"*
as a traditional bound book at:
www.1stWorldLibrary.org/purchase.asp?ISBN=1-4218-0447-6

1st World Library Literary Society is a nonprofit
organization dedicated to promoting literacy by:

- Creating a free internet library accessible from any
  computer worldwide.
- Hosting writing competitions and offering book
  publishing scholarships.

A Woman Tenderfoot
contributed by Tim, Ed & Rodney
in support of
1st World Library Literary Society

A Woman Tenderfoot
contributed by Tim, Ed & Rodney
in support of
1st World Library Literary Society

THIS BOOK IS A TRIBUTE TO THE WEST.

I have used many Western phrases as necessary to the Western setting.

I can only add that the events related really happened in the Rocky Mountains of the United States and Canada; and this is why, being a woman, I wanted to tell about them, in the hope that some going-to-Europe-in-the-summer-woman may be tempted to go West instead.

G.G.S.-T.

New York City, September 1st, 1900.

CONTENTS

I.

THE WHY OF IT.

Theoretically, I have always agreed with the Quaker wife who reformed her husband - "Whither thou goest, I go also, Dicky dear." What thou doest, I do also, Dicky dear. So when, the year after our marriage, Nimrod announced that the mountain madness was again working in his blood, and that he must go West and take up the trail for his holiday, I tucked my summer-watering-place-and-Europe-flying-trip mind away (not without regret, I confess) and cautiously tried to acquire a new vocabulary and some new ideas.

Of course, plenty of women have handled guns and have gone to the Rocky Mountains on hunting trips - but they were not among my friends. However, my imagination was good, and the outfit I got together for my first trip appalled that good man, my husband, while the number of things I had to learn appalled me.

In fact, the first four months spent 'Out West' were taken up in learning how to ride, how to dress for it, how to shoot, and how to philosophise, each of which lessons is a story in itself. But briefly, in order to come to this story, I must have a side talk with the Woman-who-goes-hunting-with-her-husband. Those not interested please omit the next chapter.

II.

OUTFIT AND ADVICE FOR THE WOMAN-WHO-GOES-HUNTING-WITH-HER-HUSBAND.

Is it really so that most women say no to camp life because they are afraid of being uncomfortable and looking unbeautiful? There is no reason why a woman should make a freak of herself even if she is going to rough it; as a matter of fact I do not rough it, I go for enjoyment and leave out all possible discomforts. There is no reason why a woman should be more uncomfortable out in the mountains, with the wild west wind for companion and the big blue sky for a roof, than sitting in a 10 by 12 whitewashed bedroom of the summer hotel variety, with the tin roof to keep out what air might be passing. A possible mosquito or gnat in the mountains is no more irritating than the objectionable personality that is sure to be forced upon you every hour at the summer hotel. The usual walk, the usual drive, the usual hop, the usual novel, the usual scandal, - in a word, the continual consciousness of self as related to dress, to manners, to position, which the gregarious living of a hotel enforces - are all right enough once in a while; but do you not get enough of such life in the winter to last for all the year?

Is one never to forget that it is not proper to wear gold

Grace Gallatin Seton-Thompson

beads with crape? Understand, I am not to be set down as having any charity for the ignoramus who would wear that combination, but I wish to record the fact that there are times, under the spell of the West, when I simply do not *care* whether there are such things as gold beads and crape; when the whole business of city life, the music, arts, drama, the pleasant friends, equally with the platitudes of things and people you care not about - civilization, in a word - when all these fade away from my thoughts as far as geographically they are, and in their place comes the joy of being at least a healthy, if not an intelligent, animal. It is a pleasure to eat when the time comes around, a good old-fashioned pleasure, and you need no dainty serving to tempt you. It is another pleasure to use your muscles, to buffet with the elements, to endure long hours of riding, to run where walking would do, to jump an obstacle instead of going around it, to return, physically at least, to your pinafore days when you played with your brother Willie. Red blood means a rose-colored world. Did you feel like that last summer at Newport or Narragansett?

So enough; come with me and learn how to be vulgarly robust.

Of course one must have clothes and personal comforts, so, while we are still in the city humor, let us order a habit suitable for riding astride. Whipcord, or a closely woven homespun, in some shade of grayish brown that harmonizes with the landscape, is best. Corduroy is pretty, if you like it, but rather clumsy. Denham will do, but it wrinkles and becomes untidy. Indeed it has been my experience that it is economy to buy the best quality of cloth you can afford, for then the garment always keeps its shape, even after hard wear, and can be cleaned and made ready for another year, and another, and another. You will need it, never fear. Once you have opened your ears, "the Red Gods" will not cease to "call for you."

In Western life you are on and off your horse at the change of a thought. Your horse is not an animate exercise-maker that John brings around for a couple of hours each morning; he is your companion, and shares the vicissitudes of your life. You even consult him on occasion, especially on matters relating to the road. Therefore your costume must look equally well on and off the horse. In meeting this requirement, my woes were many. I struggled valiantly with everything in the market, and finally, from five varieties of divided skirts and bloomers, the following practical and becoming habit was evolved.

I speak thus modestly, as there is now a trail of patterns of this habit from the Atlantic to the Pacific coast. Wherever it goes, it makes converts, especially among the wives of army officers at the various Western posts where we have been - for the majority of women in the West, and I nearly said all the sensible ones, now ride astride.

When off the horse, there is nothing about this habit to distinguish it from any trim golf suit, with the stitching up the left front which is now so popular. When on the horse, it looks, as some one phrased it, as though one were riding side saddle on both sides. This is accomplished by having the fronts of the skirt double, free nearly to the waist, and, when off the horse, fastened by patent hooks. The back seam is also open, faced for several inches, stitched and closed by patent fasteners. Snug bloomers of the same material are worn underneath. The simplicity of this habit is its chief charm; there is no superfluous material to sit upon - oh, the torture of wrinkled cloth in the divided skirt! - and it does not fly up even in a strong wind, if one knows how to ride. The skirt is four inches from the ground - it should not bell much on the sides - and about three and a half yards at the bottom, which is finished with a five-inch stitched hem.

Any style of jacket is of course suitable. One that looks well on the horse is tight fitting, with postilion back, short on hips, sharp pointed in front, with single-breasted vest of reddish leather (the habit material of brown whipcord), fastened by brass buttons, leather collar and revers, and a narrow leather band on the close-fitting sleeves. A touch of leather on the skirt in the form of a patch pocket is harmonious, but any extensive leather trimming on the skirt makes it unnecessarily heavy.

A suit of this kind should be as irreproachable in fit and finish as a tailor can make it. This is true economy, for when you return in the autumn it is ready for use as a rainy-day costume.

Once you have your habit, the next purchase should be stout, heavy soled boots, 13 or 14 inches high, which will protect the leg in walking and from the stirrup leather while riding. One needs two felt hats (never straw), one of good quality for sun or rain, with large firm brim. This is important, for if the brim be not firm the elements will soon reduce it to raglike limpness and it will flap up and down in your face as you ride. This can be borne with composure for five or ten minutes, but not for days and weeks at a time. The other felt hat may be as small and as cheap as you like.

Only see that it combines the graces of comfort and becomingness. It is for evenings, and sunless rainless days. A small brown felt, with a narrow leather band, gilt buckle, and a twist of orange veiling around the crown, is pretty for the whipcord costume.

One can do a wonderful amount of smartening up with tulle, hat pins, belts, and fancy neck ribbons, all of which comparatively take up no room and add no weight, always the first consideration. Be sure you supply yourself with a reserve of hat pins. Two devices by which they may be made to stay in the hat are here shown. The spiral can be given to any hat pin. The chain and small brooch should be used if the hat pin is of much value.

At this point, if any man, a reviewer perhaps, has delved thus far into the mysteries of feminine outfit, he will probably remark, "Why take a hat pin of much value?" to which I reply; "Why not? Can you suggest any more harmless or useful vent for woman's desire to ornament herself? And unless you want her to be that horror of horrors, a strong-minded woman, do you think you can strip her for three months of all her gewgaws and still have her filled with the proper desire to be pleasing in your eyes? No; better let her have the hat pins - and you know they really are useful - and then she will dress up to those hat pins, if it is only with a fresh neck ribbon and a daisy at her belt."

I had a man's saddle, with a narrow tree and high pommel and cantle, such as is used out West, and as I had not ridden a horse since the hazy days of my infancy, I got on the huge creature's back with everything to learn. Fear enveloped me as in a cloud during my first ride, and the possibilities of the little cow pony they put me on seemed more awe-inspiring than those of a locomotive. But I have been reading Professor William James and acquired from him the idea (I hope I do not malign him) that the accomplishment of a thing depends largely upon one's mental attitude, and this was mine all nicely taken - in New York: -

"This thing has been done before, and done well. Good; then I can do it, and *enjoy* it too."

I particularly insisted upon the latter clause - in the East. This formula is applicable in any situation. I never should have gotten through my Western experiences without it, and I advise you, my dear Woman-who-goes-hunting-with-her-husband, to take a large stock of it made up and ready for use. There is one other rule for your conduct, if you want to be a success: think what you like, but unless it is pleasant, *don't say it.*

Is it better to ride astride? I will not carry the battle ground into the East, although even here I have my opinion; but in the West, in the mountains, there can be no question that it is the *only way.* Here is an example to illustrate: Two New York women, mother and daughter, took a trip of some three hundred miles over the pathless Wind River Mountains. The mother rode astride, but the daughter preferred to exhibit her Durland Academy accomplishment, and rode side-saddle, according to the fashion set by an artful queen to hide her deformity. The advantages of health, youth and strength were all with the daughter; yet in every case on that long march it was the daughter who gave out first and compelled the pack train to halt while she and her horse rested. And the daughter was obliged to change from one horse to another, while the same horse was able to carry the mother, a slightly heavier woman, through the trip. And the back of the horse which the daughter had ridden chiefly was in such a condition from saddle galls that the animal, two months before a magnificent creature, had to be shot.

I hear you say, "But that was an extreme case." Perhaps it was, but it supports the verdict of the old mountaineers who refuse to let any horse they prize be saddled with "those gol-darned woman fripperies."

There is also another side. A woman at best is physically handicapped when roughing it with husband or brother. Then why increase that handicap by wearing trailing skirts that catch on every log and bramble, and which demand the services of at least one hand to hold up (fortunately this battle is already won), and by choosing to ride side-saddle, thus making it twice as difficult to mount and dismount by yourself, which in fact compels you to seek the assistance of a log, or stone, or a friendly hand for a lift? Western riding is not Central Park riding, nor is it Rotten Row riding. The cowboy's, or military, seat is much simpler and easier for both man and beast than the Park seat - though, of course, less stylish. That is the glory of it; you can go galloping over the prairie and uplands with never a thought that the trot is more proper, and your course, untrammelled by fenced-in roads, is straight to the setting sun or to yonder butte. And if you want a spice of danger, it is there, sometimes more than you want, in the presence of badger and gopher holes, to step into which while at high speed may mean a broken leg for your horse, perhaps a broken neck for yourself. But to return to the independence of riding astride:

Grace Gallatin Seton-Thompson

One day I was following a game trail along a very steep hank which ended a hundred feet below in a granite precipice. It had been raining and snowing in a fitful fashion, and the clay ground was slippery, making a most treacherous footing. One of the pack animals just ahead of my horse slipped, fell to his knees, the heavy pack overbalanced him, and away he rolled over and over down the slope, to be stopped from the precipice only by the happy accident of a scrub tree in the way. Frightened by this sight, my animal plunged, and he, too, lost his footing. Had I been riding side-saddle, nothing could have saved me, for the downhill was on the near side; but instead I swung out of the saddle on the off side and landed in a heap on the uphill, still clutching the bridle. That act saved my horse's life, probably, as well as my own. For the sudden weight I put on the upper side as I swung off enabled him to recover his balance just in time. I do not pretend to say that I can dismount from the off side as easily as from the near, because I am not accustomed to it. But I have frequently done it in emergencies, while a side-saddle leaves one helpless in this case as in many others.

Besides being unable to mount and dismount without assistance it is very difficult to get side-saddle broken horses, and it usually means a horse so broken in health and spirits that he does not care what is being strapped on his back and dangling on one side of him only. And to be on such an animal means that you are on the worst mount of the outfit, and I am sure that it requires little imagination on any one's part to know therein lies misery. Oh! the weariness of being the weakest of the party and the worst mounted - to be always at the tail end of the line, never to be able to keep up with the saddle horses when they start off for a canter, to expend your stock of vitality, which you should husband for larger matters, in urging your beast by voice and quirt to further exertion! Never place yourself in such a position. The former you cannot help, but you can lessen it by making use of such aids to greater independence as wearing short skirts and riding astride, and having at least as good a horse as there is in the outfit. Then you will get the pleasure from your outing that you have the right to expect - that is, if you adhere to one other bit of advice, or rather two.

The first is: See that for your camping trip is provided a man cook.

I wish that I could put a charm over the next few words so that only the woman reader could understand, but as I cannot I must repeat boldly: Dear woman who goes hunting with her husband, be sure that you have it understood that you do no cooking, or dishwashing. I think that the reason women so often dislike camping out is because the only really disagreeable part of it is left to them as a matter of course. Cooking out of doors at best is trying, and certainly you cannot be care free, camp-life's greatest charm, when you have on your mind the boiling of prunes and beans, or when tears are starting from your smoke-inflamed eyes as you broil the elk steak for dinner. No, indeed! See that your guide or your horse wrangler knows how to cook, and expects to do it. He is used to it, and, anyway, is paid for it. He is earning his living, you are taking a vacation.

Now for the second advice, which is a codicil to the above: In return for not having to potter with the food and tinware, *never complain about it*. Eat everything

Grace Gallatin Seton-Thompson

that is set before you, shut your eyes to possible dirt, or, if you cannot, leave the particular horror in question untouched, but without comment. Perhaps in desperation you may assume the role of cook yourself. Oh, foolish woman, if you do, you only exchange your woes for worse ones.

If you provide yourself with the following articles and insist upon having them reserved for you, and then let the cook furnish everything else, you will be all right: -

An aluminum plate made double for hot water. This is a very little trouble to fill, and insures a comfortable meal; otherwise, your meat and vegetables will be cold before you can eat them, and the gravy will have a thin coating of ice on it. It is always cold night and morning in the mountains. And if you do not need the plate heated you do not have to fill it; that's all. I am sure my hot-water plate often saved me from indigestion and made my meals things to enjoy instead of to endure.

Two cups and saucers of white enamel ware. They always look clean and do not break.

One silver-plated knife and fork and two teaspoons.

One folding camp chair.

N.B. - Provide your husband or brother or sister precisely the same; no more, no less.

Japanese napkins, enough to provide two a day for the party.

Two white enamel vegetable dishes.

One folding camp table.

One candle lamp, with enough candles. Then leave all the rest of the cooking outfit to your cook and trust in Providence. (If you do not approve of Providence, a full aluminum cooking outfit can be bought so that one pot or pan nests in the other, the whole very complete, compact and light.)

Come what may, you have your own particular clean hot plate, cup and saucer, knife, fork, spoon and napkin, with a table to eat from and a chair to sit on and a lamp to see by, if you are eating after dark – which often happens - and nothing else matters, but food.

If you want to be canny you will have somewhere in your own pack a modest supply of condensed soups and vegetables, a box or two of meat crackers, and three or four bottles of bouillon, to be brought out on occasions of famine. Anyway it is a comfort to know that you have provided against the wolf. So much for your part of the eating; now for the sleeping. If you do not sleep warm and comfortable at night, the joys of camping are as dust in the mouth. The most glorious morning that Nature ever produced is a weariness to the flesh of the owl-eyed. So whatever else you leave behind, be sure your sleeping arrangements are comfortable. The following is the result of three years' experience: -

A piece of waterproof brown canvas, 7 by 10 feet, bound with tape and supplied with two heavy leather straps nine feet long, with strong buckles at one end and fastened to the canvas by means of canvas loops, and one leather strap six feet long that crosses the other two at right angles.

One rubber air bed, 36 by 76 inches (don't take a narrower size or you will be uncomfortable), fitted with large size double valve at each end. This bed is six inches thick when blown full of air. Be sure that sides are inserted, thus making two seams to join together the top and bottom six inches apart. If the top and bottom are fastened directly together, your bed slopes down at the sides, which is always disagreeable.

A sleeping bag, with the canvas cover made the full 36 inches wide. This cover should hold two blanket bags of different weight, and if you are wise you will have made an eider-down bag to fit inside all of these for very cold weather. The eider bag costs about $16.00 or $18.00, but is worth it if you are going to camp out in the mountains after August. Do without one or two summer hats, but get it, for it is the keynote of camp comfort.

Then you want a lamb's wool night wrapper, a neutral grey or brown in color, a set of heavy night flannels, some heavy woollen stockings and a woollen tam o' shanter large enough to pull down over the ears. A hot-water bag, also, takes up no room and is heavenly on a freezing night when the wind is howling through the trees and snow threatens. N.B. - See that your husband or brother has a similar outfit, or he will borrow yours.

The sleeping bags should be separated and dried either by sun or fire every other day.

Always keep all your sleeping things together in your bed roll, and your husband's things together in his bed bundle. It will save you many a sigh and weary hunt in the dark and cold. The tent and such things, you can afford to leave to your guide or to luck. If one wishes to provide a tent, brown canvas is far preferable to white. It does not make a glare of light, nor does it stand out aggressively in the landscape. You have your little nightly kingdom waiting for you and can sleep cosily if nothing else is provided. Whenever possible, get your bed blown up and your sleeping bags in order on top and your sleeping things together where you can put your hands on them during the daylight, or if that is impossible, make it the first thing you do when you make camp, while the cook is getting supper. Then, as you eat supper and sit near the camp fire to keep warm, you have the sweet consciousness that over there, in the blackness is a snug little nest all ready to receive your tired self. And if some morning you want to see what you have escaped, just unscrew the air valve to your bed before you rise, and when you come down on the hard, bumpy ground, in less time than it takes to tell, you will agree with me that there is nothing so rare as resting on air. Nimrod used to play this trick on me occasionally when it was time to get up - it is more efficacious than any alarm clock - but somehow he never seemed to enjoy it when I did it to him.

For riding, it is better to carry your own saddle and bridle and to buy a saddle horse upon leaving the railroad. You can look to the guides for all the rest, such as pack saddles, pack animals, etc.

My saddle is a strong but light-weight California model; that is, with pommel and cantle on a Whitman tree. It is fitted with gun-carrying case of the same leather and saddle-bag on the skirt of each side, and has a leather roll at the back strapped on to carry an extra jacket and a slicker. (A rain-coat is most important. I use a small size of the New York mounted policemen's mackintosh, made by Goodyear. It opens front and back and has a protecting cape for the hands.) The saddle has also small pommel bags in which are matches, compass, leather thongs, knife and a whistle (this last in case I get lost), and there are rings and strings in which other bundles such as lunch can be attached while on the march. A horsehair army saddle blanket saves the animal's back. Nimrod's saddle is exactly like mine, only with longer and larger stirrups.

You have now your personal things for eating, sleeping and riding. It remains but to clothe yourself and you are ready to start. Provide yourself with two or three champagne baskets covered with brown waterproof canvas, with stout handles at each end and two leather straps going round the basket to buckle the lid down, and a stronger strap going lengthwise over all. Or if you do not mind a little more expense, telescopes made of leatheroid, about 22 inches long, 11 inches wide and 9 inches deep, with the lower corners rounded so they will not stick into the horse, and fitted with straps and handles, make the ideal travelling case; for they can be shipped from place to place on the railroad and can be packed, one on each side of a horse. They are much to be preferred to the usual Klondike bag for convenience in packing and unpacking one's things and in protecting them.

It is hardly necessary to say that clothes have to be kept down to the limit of comfort. Into the telescopes or baskets should go warm flannels, extra pair of heavy boots, several flannel shirt waists, extra riding habit and bloomers, fancy neck ribbons and a belt or two - for why look worse than your best at any time? - a long warm cloak and a chamois jacket for cold weather, snow overshoes, warm gloves and mittens too, and some woollen stockings. Be sure you take flannels. This is the advice of one who never wears them at any other time. A veil or two is very useful, as the wind is often high and biting, and I was much annoyed with wisps of hair around my eyes, and also with my hair coming down while on horseback, until I hit upon the device of tying a brown liberty silk veil over the hair and partially over the ears before putting on a sombrero. This veil was not at all unbecoming, being the same color as my hair, and it served the double purpose of keeping unruly locks in order and keeping my ears warm. A hair net is also useful.

Then you must not forget a rubber bath tub, a rubber wash basin, sponge, towels, soap, and toilet articles generally, including camphor ice for chapped lips and pennyroyal vaseline salve for insect bites. A brown linen case is invaluable to hold all these toilet necessaries, so that you can find them quickly. A sewing kit should be supplied, a flask of whiskey, and a small "first-aid" outfit; a bottle of Perry Davis pain killer or Pond's extract; but no more bottles than must be, as they are almost sure to be broken. In your husband's box, ammunition takes the place of toilet articles. I shall pass over the guns with the bare mention that I use a 30.30 Winchester, smokeless. For railroad purposes all this outfit for two goes into two trunks and a box - one trunk for all the bedding and night things: the other for all the clothing, guns, ammunition, eating things, and incidentals. The box holds the saddles, bridles, and horse things.

In a pack train, the bed-rolls, weighing about fifty pounds each, go on either side of one horse, and the telescopes on each side of another horse - in both cases not a full load, and leaving room on the top of the pack for a tent and other camp things. The saddles, of course, go on the saddle horses. The cost of such an outfit, in New York, is about two hundred dollars each; but it lasts for years and brings you in large returns in health and consequent happiness.

I am willing to wager my horsehair rope (specially designed for keeping off snakes) that a summer in the Rockies would enable you to cheat time of at least two years, and you would come home and join me in the ranks of converts from the usual summer sort of thing. Will you try it? If you do, how you will pity your unfortunate friends who have never known what it is to sleep on the south side of a sage brush, and honestly say in the morning, "It is wonderful how well I am feeling."

But to begin: -

III.

THE FIRST PLUNGE OF
THE WOMAN TENDERFOOT.

It was about midnight in the end of August when Nimrod and I tumbled off the train at Market Lake, Idaho. Next morning, after a comfortable night's rest at the "hotel," our rubber beds, sleeping bags, saddles, guns, clothing, and ourselves were packed into a covered wagon, drawn by four horses, and we started for Jackson's Hole in charge of a driver who knew the road perfectly. At least, that was what he said, so of course he must have known it. But his memory failed him sadly the first day out, which reduced him to the necessity of inquiring of the neighbours. As these were unsociably placed from thirty to fifty miles apart, there were many times when the little blind god of chance ruled our course.

We put up for the night at Rexburgh, after forty long miles of alkali dust. The Mormon religion has sent a thin arm up into that country, and the keeper of the log building he called a hotel was of that faith. The history of our brief stay there belongs properly to the old torture days of the Inquisition, for the Mormon's possessions of living creatures were many, and his wives and children were the least of them.

Another day of dust and long hard miles over gradually rising hills, with the huge mass of the Tetons looming ever nearer, and the next day we climbed the Teton Pass.

There is nothing extraordinary about climbing the Teton Pass - to tell about. We just went up, and then we went down. It took six horses half a day to draw us up the last mile - some twenty thousand seconds of conviction on my part (unexpressed, of course; see side talk) that the next second would find us dashed to everlasting splinters. And it took ten minutes to get us down!

Of the two, I preferred going up. If you have ever climbed a greased pole during Fourth of July festivities in your grandmother's village, you will understand.

When we got to the bottom there was something different. Our driver informed us that in two hours we should be eating dinner at the ranch house in Jackson's Hole, where we expected to stop for a while to recuperate from the past year's hard grind and the past two weeks of travel. This was good news, as it was then five o'clock and our midday meal had been light - despite the abundance of coffee, soggy potatoes, salt pork, wafer slices of meat swimming in grease, and evaporated apricots wherein some nice red ants were banqueting.

"We'll just cross the Snake River, and then it'll be plain sailing," he said. Perhaps it was so. I was inexperienced in the West. This was what followed: - Closing the door on the memory of my recent perilous passage, I prepared to be calm inwardly, as I like to think I was outwardly. The Snake River is so named because for every mile it goes ahead it retreats half way alongside to see how well it has been done. I mention this as a pleasing instance of a name that really describes the thing named. But this is after knowledge.

About half past five, we came to a rolling tumbling yellow stream where the road stopped abruptly with a horrid drop into water that covered the hubs of the wheels. The current was strong, and the horses had to struggle hard to gain the opposite bank. I began to thank my patron saint that the Snake River was crossed.

Crossed? Oh, no! A narrow strip of pebbly road, and the high willows suddenly parted to disclose another stream like the last, but a little deeper, a little wider, a little worse. We crossed it. I made no comments.

At the third stream the horses rebelled. There are many things four horses can do on the edge of a wicked looking river to make it uncomfortable, but at last they had to go in, plunging madly, and dragging the wagon into the stream nearly broadside, which made at least one in the party consider the frailty of human contrivances when matched against a raging flood.

Soon there was another stream. I shall not describe it. When we eventually got through it, the driver stopped his horses to rest, wiped his brow, went around the wagon and pulled a few ropes tighter, cut a willow stick and mended his broken whip, gave a hitch to his trousers, and remarked as he started the horses:

"Now, when we get through the Snake River on here a piece, we'll be all right."

"I thought we had been crossing it for the past hour," I was feminine enough to gasp.

"Oh, yes, them's forks of it; but the main stream's on ahead, and it's mighty treacherous, too," was the calm reply.

When we reached the Snake River, there was no doubt that the others were mere forks. Fortunately, Joe Miller and his two sons live on the opposite bank, and make a living by helping people escape destruction from the mighty waters. Two men waved us back from the place where our driver was lashing his horses into the rushing current, and guided us down stream some distance. One of them said:

"This yere ford changes every week, but I reckon you might try here."

We did.

Had my hair been of the dramatic kind that realises situations, it would have turned white in the next ten minutes. The water was over the horses' backs immediately, the wagon box was afloat, and we were being borne rapidly down stream in the boiling seething flood, when the wheels struck a shingly bar which gave the horses a chance to half swim, half plunge. The two men, who were on horseback, each seized one of the leaders, and kept his head pointed for a cut in the bank, the only place where we could get out.

Everything in the wagon was afloat. A leather case with a forty dollar fishing rod stowed snugly inside slipped quietly off down stream. I rescued my camera from the same fate just in time. Overshoes, wraps, field glasses, guns, were suddenly endowed with motion. Another moment and we should surely have sunk, when the horses, by a supreme effort, managed to scramble on to the bank, but were too exhausted to draw more than half of the wagon after them, so that it was practically on end in the water, our outfit submerged, of course, and ourselves reclining as gracefully as possible on the backs of the seats.

Had anything given away then, there might have been a tragedy. The two men immediately fastened a rope to the tongue of the wagon, and each winding an end around the pommel of his saddle, set his cow pony pulling. Our horses made another effort, and up we came out of the water, wet, storm tossed, but calm. Oh, yes - calm! After that, earth had no terrors for me; the worst road that we could bump over was but an incident. I was not surprised that it grew dark very soon, and that we blundered on and on for hours in the night until the near wheeler just lay down in the dirt, a dark spot in the dark road, and our driver, after coming back from a tour of inspection on foot, looked worried. I mildly asked if we would soon cross Snake River, but his reply was an admission that he was lost. There was nothing visible but the twinkling stars and a dim outline of the grim Tetons. The prospect was excellent for passing the rest of the night where we were, famished, freezing, and so tired I could hardly speak.

But Nimrod now took command. His first duty, of course, being a man, was to express his opinion of the driver in terms plain and comprehensive; then he loaded his rifle and fired a shot. If there were any mountaineers around, they would understand the signal and answer.

We waited. All was silent as before. Two more horses dropped to the ground. Then he sent another loud report into the darkness. In a few moments we thought we heard a distant shout, then the report of a gun not far away.

Nimrod mounted the only standing horse and went in the direction of the sound. Then followed an interminable silence. I hallooed, but got no answer. The wildest fears for Nimrod's safety tormented me. He had fallen into a gully, the horse had thrown him, *he* was lost.

Then I heard a noise and listened eagerly. The driver said it was a coyote howling up on the mountain. At last voices did come to me from out of the blackness, and Nimrod returned with a man and a fresh horse. The man was no other than the owner of the house for which we were searching, and in ten minutes I was drying myself by his fireplace, while his hastily aroused wife was preparing a midnight supper for us.

To this day, I am sure that driver's worst nightmare is when he lives over again the time when he took a tenderfoot and his wife into Jackson's Hole, and, but for the tenderfoot, would have made them stay out overnight, wet, famished, frozen, within a stone's throw of the very house for which they were looking.

IV.

WHICH TREATS OF THE IMPS AND MY ELK.

"If you want to see elk, you just follow up the road till you strike a trail on the left, up over that hog's back, and that will bring you in a mile or so on to a grassy flat, and in two or three miles more you come to a lake back in the mountains."

Mrs. Cummings, the speaker, was no ordinary woman of Western make. She had been imported from the East by her husband three years before. She had been 'forelady in a corset factory,' when matrimony had enticed her away, and the thought that walked beside her as she baked, and washed, and fed the calves, was that some day she would go 'back East.' And this in spite of the fact that for those parts she was very comfortable.

Her log house was the largest in the country, barring Captain Jones's, her nearest neighbour, ten miles up at Jackson's Lake, and his was a hotel. Hers could boast of six rooms and two clothes' closets. The ceilings were white muslin to shut off the rafters, the sitting room had wall-paper and a rag carpet, and in one corner was the post-office.

The United States Government Post-office of Deer,

Wyoming, took up two compartments of Mrs. Cummings' writing desk, and she was called upon to be postmistress fifteen minutes twice a week, when the small boy, mounted on a tough little pony, happened around with the leather bag which carried the mail to and from Jackson, thirty miles below.

"I'd like some elk meat mighty well for dinner," Mrs. Cummings continued, as she leaned against the kitchen door and watched us mount our newly acquired horses, "but you won't find game around here without a guide - Easterners never do."

Nimrod and I started off in joyous mood. The secret of it, the fascination of the wild life, was revealed to me. At last I understood why the birds sing. The glorious exhilaration of the mountains, the feeling that life is a rosy dream, and that all the worry and the fever and the fret of man's making is a mere illusion that has faded away into the past, and is not worth while; that the real life is to be free, to fly over the grassy mountain meadow with never a limitation of fence or house, with the eternal peaks towering around you, terrible in their grandeur and vastness, yet inviting.

We struck the trail all right, we thought, but it soon disappeared and we had to govern our course by imagination, an uncertain guide at best. We got into dreadful tangles of timber; the country was all strange, and the trees spread over the mountain for miles, so that it was like trying to find the way under a blanket; but we kept on riding our horses over fallen logs and squeezing them between trees, all the time keeping a sharp watch over them, for they were fresh and scary.

Finally, after three hours' hard climbing, we emerged

from the forest on to a great bare shoulder of the mountain, from which the whole country around, vast and beautiful, could be seen. We took bearings and tried to locate that lake, and we finally decided that a wooded basin three miles away looked likely to contain it.

In order to get to it, we had to cross a wooded ravine, very steep and torn out by a recent cloudburst. We rode the horses down places that I shudder in remembering, and I had great trouble in keeping away from the front feet of my horse as I led him, especially when there were little gullies that had to be jumped.

It was exciting enough, and hard work, too, every nerve on a tingle and one's heart thumping with the unwonted exercise at that altitude; but oh, the glorious air, the joy of life and motion that was quite unknown to my reception and theatre-going self in the dim far away East!

We searched for that lake all day, and at nightfall went home confident that we could find it on the morrow.

Mrs. Cummings' smile clearly expressed 'I told you so,' and she remarked as she served supper: "When my husband comes home next week, he will take you where you can find game."

The next morning we again took some lunch in the saddle bag and started for that elusive spot we had christened Cummings' Lake. About three o'clock we found it - a beautiful patch of water in the heart of the forest, nestling like a jewel, back in the mountains.

We picketed the horses at a safe distance, so that they

could not be seen or heard from the lake. At one end the shore sloped gradually into the water, and here Nimrod discovered many tracks of elk, a few deer, and one set of black bear. He said the lake was evidently a favourite drinking place, that a band of elk had been coming daily to water, and that, according to their habits, they ought to come again before dusk.

So we concealed ourselves on a little bluff to the right and waited. The sun had begun to cast long lines on the earth, and the little circle of water was already in shadow when Nimrod held up his finger as a warning for silence. We listened. We were so still that the whole world seemed to be holding its breath.

I heard a faint noise as of a snapping branch, then some light thuds along the ground, and to the left of us out of the dark forest, a dainty creature flitted along the trail and playfully splashed into the water. Six others of her sisters followed her, with two little ones, and they were all splashing about in the water like so many sportive mermaids when their lordly master appeared - a fine bull elk who seemed to me, as he sedately approached the edge of the lake, to be nothing but horns.

I shall never forget the picture of this family at home - the quiet lake encircled by forest and towered over by mountains; the gentle graceful creatures full of life playing about in the water, now drinking, now splashing it in cooling showers upon one another; the solicitude of a mother that her young one should come to no harm; and then the head of them all proceeding with dignity to bathe with his harem.

Had I to do again what followed, I hope I should act

differently. Nimrod was watching them with a rapt expression, quite forgetful of the rifle in his hands, when I, who had never seen anything killed, touched his arm and whispered: "Shoot, shoot now, if you are going to."

The report of the rifle rang out like a cannon. The does fled away as if by magic. The stag tried also to get to shore, but the ball had inflicted a wound which partially paralysed his hindquarters. At the sight of the blood and the big fellow's struggles to get away, the horror of the thing swept over me. "Oh, kill him, kill him!" I wailed. "Don't let him suffer!"

But here the hunter in Nimrod answered: "If I kill him now, I shall never be able to get him. Wait until he gets out of the water."

The next few seconds, with that struggling thing in the water, seemed an eternity of agony to me. Then another loud bang caused the proud head with its weight of antlers to sink to the wet bank never to rise again.

Later, as I dried my tears, I asked Nimrod:

"Where is the place to aim if you want to kill an animal instantly, so that he will not suffer, and never know what hit him?"

"The best place is the shoulder." He showed me the spot on his elk.

"But wouldn't he suffer at all?"

"Well, of course, if you hit him in the brain, he will

never know; but that is a very fine shot. Your target is only an inch or two, here between the eye and the ear, and the head moves more than the body. But," he said, "you would not kill an elk after the way you have wept over this one?"

"If - if I were sure he would not suffer, I might kill just one," I said, conscious of my inconsistencies. My woman's soul revolted, and yet I was out West for all the experiences that the life could give me, and I knew, if the chance came just right, that one elk would be sacrificed to that end.

The next day, much to Mrs. Cummings' surprise, we had elk steak, the most delicious of meat when properly cooked. The next few days slipped by. We were always in the open air, riding about in those glorious mountains, and it was the end of the week when a turn of the wheel brought my day.

First, it becomes necessary to confide in you. Fear is a very wicked companion who, since nursery days, had troubled me very little; but when I arrived out West, he was waiting for me, and, so that I need never be without him, he divided himself into a band of little imps.

Each imp had a special duty, and never left me until he had been crushed in silent but terrible combat. There was the imp who did not like to be alone in the mountains, and the imp who was sure he was going to be lost in those wildernesses, and the imp who quaked at the sight of a gun, and the imp who danced a mad fierce dance when on a horse. All these had been conquered, or at least partially reduced to subjection, but the imp who sat on the saddle pommel when there was a ditch or stream to be jumped had hitherto obliged me to dismount and get over the space on foot.

This morning, when we came to a nasty boggy place, with several small water cuts running through it, I obeyed the imp with reluctance. Well, we got over it - Blondey, the imp, and I - with nothing worse than wet feet and shattered nerves.

I attempted to mount, and had one foot in the stirrup and one hand on the pommel, when Blondey started. Like the girl in the song, I could not get up, I could not get down, and although I had hold of the reins, I had no free hand to pull them in tighter, and you may be sure the imp did not help me. Blondey, realising there was something wrong, broke into a wild gallop across country, but I clung on, expecting every moment the saddle would turn, until I got my foot clear from the stirrup. Then I let go just as Blondey was gathering himself together for another ditch.

I was stunned, but escaped any serious hurt. Nimrod was a great deal more undone than I. He had not dared to go fast for fear of making Blondey go faster, and he now came rushing up, with the fear of death upon his face and the most terrible swears on his lips.

Although a good deal shaken, I began to laugh, the combination was so incongruous. Nimrod rarely swears, and was now quite unconscious what his tongue was doing. Upon being assured that all was well, he started after Blondey and soon brought him back to me; but while he was gone the imp and I had a mortal combat.

I did up my hair, rearranged my habit, and, rejecting

Nimrod's offer of his quieter horse, remounted Blondey. We all jumped the next ditch, but the shock was too much for the imp in his weakened condition; he tumbled off the pommel, and I have never seen him since.

Our course lay along the hills on the east bank of Snake River that day. We discovered another beautiful sapphire lake in a setting of green hills. Several ducks were gliding over its surface. We watched them, in concealment of course, and we saw a fish hawk capture his dinner. Then we quietly continued along the ridge of a high bluff until we came to an outstretched point, where beneath us lay the Snake Valley with its fickle-minded river winding through.

The sun was just dropping behind the great Tetons, massed in front of us across the valley. We sat on our horses motionless, looking at the peaceful and majestic scene, when out from the shadows on the sandy flats far below us came a dark shadow, and then leisurely another and another. They were elk, two bulls and a doe, grazing placidly in a little meadow surrounded by trees.

We kept as still as statues.

Nimrod said. "There is your chance."

"Yes," I echoed, "here is my chance."

We waited until they passed into the trees again. Then we dismounted. Nimrod handed me the rifle, saying:

"There are seven shots in it. I will stay behind with the horses."

I took the gun without a word and crept down the mountain side, keeping under cover as much as possible. The sunset quiet surrounded me; the deadly quiet of but one idea - to creep upon that elk and kill him - possessed me. That gradual painful drawing nearer to my prey seemed a lifetime. I was conscious of nothing to the right, or to the left of me; only of what I was going to do. There were pine woods and scrub brush and more woods. Then, suddenly, I saw him standing by the river about to drink. I crawled nearer until I was within one hundred and fifty yards of him, when at the snapping of a twig he raised his head with its crown of branching horn. He saw nothing, so turned again to drink.

Now was the time. I crawled a few feet nearer and raised the deadly weapon. The stag turned partly away from me. In another moment he would be gone. I sighted along the metal barrel and a terrible bang went booming through the dim secluded spot. The elk raised his proud, antlered head and looked in my direction. Another shot tore through the air. Without another move the animal dropped where he stood. He lay as still as the stones beside him, and all was quiet again in the twilight.

I sat on the ground where I was and made no attempt to go near him. So that was all. One instant a magnificent breathing thing, the next - nothing.

Death had been so sudden. I had no regret, I had no triumph - just a sort of wonder at what I had done - a surprise that the breath of life could be taken away so easily.

Meanwhile, Nimrod had become alarmed at the long

Grace Gallatin Seton-Thompson

silence, and, tying the horses, had followed me down the mountain. He was nearly down when he heard the shots, and now came rushing up.

"I have done it," I said in a dull tone, pointing at the dark, quiet object on the bank.

"You surely have."

Nimrod paced the distance - it was one hundred and thirty-five yards - as we went up to the elk. How beautiful his coat was, glossy and shaded in browns, and those great horns - eleven points - that did not seem so big now to my eyes.

Nimrod examined the carcass.

"You are an apt pupil," he said. "You put a bullet through his heart and another through his brain."

"Yes," I said; "he never knew what killed him." But I felt no glory in the achievement.

V.

LOST IN THE MOUNTAINS.

Have you ever been lost in the mountains? - not the peaceful, cultivated child hills of the Catskills, but in real mountains, where the first outpost of civilisation, a lonely ranch house, is two weeks' travel away, and where that stream on your left is bound for the Pacific Ocean, and that stream on your right over there will, after four thousand miles, find its way into the Atlantic Ocean, and where the air you breathe is twelve thousand feet above those seas? I have.

The situation is naturally one you would not fish out of the grab bag of fate if you could avoid it. When you suddenly find it on your hands, however, there is only one thing to do - keep your nerve, grasp it firmly, and look at it closely. If you have a horse and a gun and a cartridge, it is not so bad. I had these and I had better than all these, I had Nimrod - but only half of Nimrod. The working half was chained up by my fears, for such is the power of a woman. I will explain. In crossing over the Continental Divide of the Rocky Mountains, we were guests in the pack train of a man who was equally at home in a New York drawing-room or on a Wyoming bear hunt, and he had made mountain travelling a fine art. Besides ourselves, there were the horse wrangler, the cook (of whom you shall hear later), and sixteen horses, and we started from Jackson's Lake for the Big Horn Basin, several hundred miles over the pathless uninhabited mountains.

No one who has not tried it knows how difficult it is for two or three men to keep so many pack animals in line, with no pathway to guide; and once they are started going nicely, it is nothing short of a calamity to stop them, especially when it is necessary to cover a certain number of miles before nightfall in order that they may have feed.

We were on the Pacific side of the Wind River Divide, and must get to the top that night. The horses were travelling nicely up the difficult ascent, so when Nimrod got his feet wet crossing a stream about noon, he and I thought we would just stop and have a little lunch, dry the shoes, and catch up with the pack train in half an hour.

From the minute the last horse vanished out of sight behind a rock, desolation settled upon me. That slender line of living beings somewhere on ahead was the only link between us and civilisation - civilisation which I understood, which was human and touchable - and the awful vastness of those endless peaks, wherein lurked a hundred dangers, and which seemed made but to annihilate me.

Of course, the fire would not burn, and the shoes would not dry. Blondey wandered off and had to be brought back, and it seemed an age before we were again in the saddle, following the trail the animals had made.

But Nimrod was blithe and unconcerned, so I made no sign of the craven soul within me. For an hour or two we followed the trail, urging our horses as much as possible, but the ascent was difficult, and we could not gain on the speed of the pack train. Then the trail was lost in a gully where the animals had gone in every direction to get through. My nerves were now on the rack of suspense.

Where were they? Surely, we must have passed them! We were on the wrong trail, perhaps going away from them at every step!

The screws of fear grew tighter every moment during the following hours. Nimrod soon found what he considered to be the trail, and we proceeded.

At last we got to the top. No sign of them. I could have screamed aloud; a great wave of soul destroying fear encompassed me - wild black fear. I could not reason it out. We were lost!

Nimrod scoffed at me. The track was still plain, he said; but I could not read the hieroglyphics at my feet, and there was no room in my mind for confidence or hope. Fear filled it all.

There we were with the mighty forces of the insensate world around, so pitiless, so silently cruel, it seemed to my city-bred soul. It was the spot where Nature spread her wonders before us, one tiny spring dividing its waters east and west for the Atlantic and Pacific oceans, for this was the highest point.

We attempted to cross that hateful divide, that at another time might have looked so beautiful, when suddenly Nimrod's horse plunged withers deep in a bog, and in his struggles to get out threw Nimrod head first from the saddle into the mud, where he lay quite still.

I faced the horror of death at that moment. Of course, this was what I had been expecting, but had not been able to put into words. Nimrod killed! My other fears dwindled away before this one, or, rather, it seemed to wrap them in itself, as in a cloak. For an instant I could not move - there alone with a dead or wounded man on that awful mountain top.

But here was an emergency where I could do something besides blindly follow another's lead. I caught the frightened animal as it dashed out of the treacherous place (to be horseless is almost a worse fate than to be wounded), and Nimrod, who was little hurt, quickly recovered and managed to scramble to dry ground, and again into the saddle.

Forcing our tired horses onward, we again found a trail, supposedly the right one, but there was that haunting fear that it was not. For the only signs were the bending of the grass and the occasional rubbing of the trees where the animals had passed. And these might have been done by a band of elk.

It was growing dusk and still no pack train in sight. No criminal on trial for his life could have felt more wretchedly apprehensive than I. At last we came to a stream. Nimrod, who had dismounted to examine more closely, said:

"The trail turns off here, but it is very dim in the grass."

"Where?" I asked, anxiously.

He pointed to the ground. I could make out nothing. "Oh, let us hurry! They must have gone on."

"I think it would be safer to follow these tracks for a time at least, to see where they come out. There are some tracks across the stream there, but they are older and dimmer and might have been made by elk."

"Oh, do go on! Surely the tracks across the stream must be the ones." To go on, on, and hurry, was my one thought, my one cry.

Nimrod yielded. Thus I and my wild fear betrayed the hunter's instinct. We went on for many weary minutes. We lost all tracks. Then Nimrod fired a shot into the air. He would not do it before, because he said we were not lost, and that there was no need for worry - worry, when for hours blind fear had held me in torture!

There was no answer to the shot.

In five minutes he fired again. Then we heard a report, very faint. I would not believe that I had heard it at all. I raised my gun and fired. This time a shot rattled through the branches overhead, unpleasantly near. It was clearly from behind us. We turned, and after another interchange of shots, the cook appeared.

I was too exhausted to be glad, but a feeling of relief glided over me. He led us to the stream where Nimrod had wanted to turn off, and from there we were quickly in camp, very much to our host's relief. I dropped at the foot of a tree, and said nothing for an hour - my companions were men, so I did not have to talk if I could not - then I arose as usual and was ready for supper.

Of course, Nimrod was blamed for not being a better mountaineer. 'He ought to have seen that broken turf by the trail,' or those 'blades of fresh pulled grass in the pine fork.' How could they know that a woman and her fears had hampered him at every step, especially as you see there was no need?

Always regulate your fears according to the situation, and then you will not go into the valley of the shadow of death, when you are only lost in the mountains.

VI.

THE COOK.

I had but a bare speaking acquaintance with the grim silent mountaineer who was cook to our party. Two days after he had appeared like an angel of heaven on our gloomy path I had an opportunity of knowing him better. I quote from my journal:

Camp Jim, Shoshone Range, September 23: They left me alone in camp today. No, the cook was there. They left me the cook for protection against the vast solitude, the mighty grandeur of the mountains, and the possible, but improbable, bear. Nice man, that cook - he confessed with pride to many robberies and three murders! Only a month before engaging as cook on this trip, he had been serving a life term for murder; but had been released through some political 'pull.'

Our host, in company with another game warden, had discovered him in the mountains, where he had gone immediately from the penitentiary and resumed his unlawful life of killing game. But he had hidden his prizes so effectively that there was no evidence but his own, which, of course, is not accepted in law. Thus he welcomed these two men of justice to his camp, told graphically of his killing - then offered them a smoke, smiling the while at their discomfiture.

Grace Gallatin Seton-Thompson

Both his face and hands were scarred from many bar room encounters, and he unblushingly dated most of his remarks by the period when he 'was rusticatin' in the Pen.' He had brought his own bed and saddle and pack horses on the trip so that he could 'cut loose' from the party in case 'things got too hot' for him.

Such was the cook.

Immediately after breakfast Nimrod and our host equipped themselves for the day's hunt, and went off in opposite directions, like *Huck Finn* and *Tom Sawyer* on the occasion of their memorable first smoke.

Our camp was beside a rushing brook in a little glade that was tucked at the foot of towering mountains where no man track had been for years, if ever. Around us sighed the mighty pines of the limitless forest. Hundreds of miles away, beyond the barrier of nature, were human hives weary of the noise and strife of their own making. Here, alone in the solitudes, were two human atoms wandering on the trail of the hunted, and - the cook and I.

I sat on my rubber bed in the tent and thought - there was nothing else to do - and was cold, cold from the outside in, and from the inside out. There wasn't a thing alive, not even myself - no one but the cook.

Outside, I could hear him washing the breakfast tinware, and whistling some kind of a jiggling tune that ran up and down me like a shiver. This went on for an eternity.

Suddenly it stopped, and I heard the faintest crunch on the thin layer of snow and the rattling of more snow as it slid off my tent from a blow that had been struck on the outside.

I jumped to the door of the tent. It was the cook.

"Purty cold in there, ain't it? You'd a good sight better come to the fire. Ain't you got a slicker?"

I put on a mackintosh and overshoes and went to the fire. The weather was now indulging in a big flake snow that slid stealthily to the ground and disappeared into water on whatever obstacle it found there. It found me. The cook was cleaning knives - the cooking knives, the eating knives, and a full set of hunting knives, long and short, slim and broad, all sharp and efficacious.

He handled them lovingly, rubbed off some blood rust here and there, and occasionally whetted one to a still more razor edge and threw it into a near by tree, where it stuck, quivering.

There was no conversation, but I did not feel forgotten.

I turned my back on the cook and gazed into the fire, a miserable smouldering affair, and speculated on why I had never before noticed how much spare time there was in a minute. It may have been five of these spacious minutes, it may have been fifteen, that had passed away when the cook approached me. I could *feel* him coming. He came very close to me - and to the fire.

He put on some beans.

Then he went away, and there were many more

minutes, many more.

Then something touched my arm. At last it had come (what we expect, if it be disagreeable, usually does come). I never moved a muscle. This time the pressure on my arm was unmistakable. I turned quickly and saw - the cook - with a gun!

The cook, gun, knives, fire, snow, and stars danced a mad jig before me for an instant. Then the cook suddenly resumed his proper position, and I saw that his disengaged hand was held in an attitude of warning for silence. He pointed off into the woods and appeared to be listening. Soon I thought I heard a snapping of a branch away off up the mountain.

"Bear," the cook whispered. "Follow me."

I followed. It was hard work to get over logs and stones without noise, in a long mackintosh, and, besides, I wished that I had brought a gun. I should have felt more comfortable about both man and beast. I struggled on for a while, when the thought suddenly struck home that if I went farther I should not be able to find my way back to camp. Everything is relative, and those empty tents and smouldering fire seemed a haven of security compared to the situation of being unarmed, and lost in the wilderness - with the cook.

I watched my chance and sneaked back to camp to get a gun. I was willing to believe the cook's bear story, but I wanted a gun. When I got to camp there were many good reasons for not going back.

After a time I heard two shots close at hand, and soon the cook appeared. He said he could not find the bear's track, and lost me, so thought he had better look me up and be on hand in case I had returned to camp, and the bear should come.

I thanked the cook for his solicitude.

To while away the time, I put up a target and commenced practising with a 30-30 rifle at fifty yards range.

I shot very badly.

The cook obligingly interested himself in my performance and kept tally on my aim, pointing out to me when it was high, when it was low, to the right or to the left.

Then he took his six shooter and put a half dozen bullets in the bull's-eye offhand.

I lost my interest in shooting.

The cook gave me some lunch, and while I was eating he stood before the fire looking at it through the fingers of his. Outstretched hand, with a queer squint in his cold gray eyes, as though sighting along a rifle barrel, while a cigarette hung limply from his mouth.

Then in response to a winning smile (after all, a woman's best weapon) he opened the floodgates of his thoughts and poured into my ears a succession of bloodcurdling adventures over which the big, big 'I' had dominated. "Yes," he said musingly of his *second* murder, as he removed his squint from the fire to me, and a ghost of a smile played around his lips; "yes, it took six shots to keep him quiet, and you could have covered all the holes with a cap box - and his pard nearly got me."

"That was the year I lost my pard, Dick Elsen. We was at camp near Fort Fetterman. We called a man 'Red' - his name was Jim Capse. Drink was at the bottom of it. Red he sees my pard passing a saloon, and he says, 'Hello, where did you come from? Come and have a drink!' Pard says, 'No, I don't want nothing!' 'Oh, come along and have a drink!' Dick says, 'No, thanks, pard, I'm not drinking to-night.' 'Well, I guess you'll have a drink with me'; and Red pulls out his six shooter. Dick wasn't quick enough about throwing up his hands, and he gets killed. Then Irish Mike says to Red, 'You better hit the breeze,' but we ketched him - a telegraph pole was handy - I says, 'Have you got anything to say?' 'You write to my mother and tell her that, a horse fell on me. Don't tell her that I got hung,' Red says; and we swung him."

By the time he had thus proudly stretched out his three dead men before my imagination, in a setting of innumerable shooting scraps and horse stealings, the hunters returned - my day with the multi-murderous cook was over - and nothing had happened.

It is only fair to quote Nimrod's reply to one who criticised him for leaving me thus:

"Humph! Do you think I don't know those wild mountaineers? They are perfectly chivalrous, and I could feel a great deal safer in leaving my wife in care of that desperado than with one of your Eastern dudes."

VII.

AMONG THE CLOUDS.

Many a time as a child I used to lie on my back in the grass and stare far into the wide blue sky above. It seemed so soft, so caressing, so far away, and yet so near. Then, perhaps, a tiny woolly cloud would drift across its face, meet another of its kind, then another and another, until the massed up curtain hid the playful blue, and amid grayness and chill, where all had been so bright, I would hurry under shelter to avoid the storm. That, outside of fairy books, an earthbound being could actually be in a cloud, was beyond my imagination. Indeed, it seems strange now, and were it not for the absence of a cherished quirt, I should be ready to think that my cloud experience had been a dream.

The day before, we had been in a great hurry to cross the Wind River Divide before a heavy snowfall made travel difficult, if not impossible. We had no wish to be snowbound for the winter in those wilds, with only two weeks' supply of food, and it was for this same reason we had not stopped to hunt that grizzly who had left a fourteen inch track over on Wiggins' Creek - the same being Wahb of the Big Horn Basin, about whom I shall have something to say later.

We were now camped in a little valley whose creek bubbled pleasantly under the ice. Having cleared away three feet of snow for our tents, we decided to rest a day or two and hunt, as we were within two days' easy travel of the first ranch house.

It was cold and snowy when Nimrod and I started out next morning to look for mountain sheep. I followed Nimrod's horse for several miles as in a trance, the white flakes falling silently around me, and wondered how it would be possible for any human being to find his way back to camp; but I had been taught my lesson, and kept silent.

I even tried to make mental notes of various rocks and trees we passed, but it was hopeless. They all looked alike to me. In a city, no matter how big or how strange, I can find home unerringly, and Nimrod is helpless as a babe. In the mountains it is different. When I finally raised my eyes from the horse's tail in front, it was because the tail and the horse belonging to it had stopped suddenly.

We were in the middle of a brook. It is highly unpleasant to be stopped in the middle of an icy brook when your horse's feet break through the ice at each step, and you cannot be sure how deep the water is, nor how firm the bottom he is going to strike, especially as ice-covered brooks are Blondey's pet abhorrence, and the uncertainty of my progress, was emphasised by Blondey's attempts to cross on one or two feet instead of four.

However, I looked dutifully in the direction Nimrod indicated and saw a long line of elk heads peering over the ridge in front and showing darkly against the snow.

They were not startled.

Those inquisitive heads, with ears alert, looked at us for some time, and then leisurely moved out of sight. We scrambled out of the stream and commenced ascending the mountain after them. The damp snow packed on Blondey's hoofs, so that he was walking on snowballs. When these got about five inches high, they would drop off and begin again. It is needless to say that these varying snowballs did not help Blondey's sure-footedness, especially as the snow was just thick enough to conceal the treacherous slaty rocks beneath. For the first time I understood the phrase, to be 'all balled up.'

Between being ready to clear myself from the saddle and jump off on the up side, in case Blondey should fall, and keeping in sight of the tail of the other horse, I had given no attention to the landscape.

Suddenly I lost Nimrod, and everything was swallowed up in a dark misty vapour that cut me off from every object. Even Blondey's nose and the ground at my feet were blurred. Regardless of possibly near-by elk, I raised a frightened, yell. My voice swirled around me and dropped. I tried again, but the sound would not carry.

The icy vapour swept through me - a very lonely forlorn little being indeed. I just clung to the saddle, trusting to Blondey's instinct to follow the other animal, and tried to enjoy the fact that I was getting a new sensation. Even when one could see, every step was treacherous, but in that black fog I might as well have been blind and deaf. Then Blondey dislodged some loose rock, and went sliding down the mountain with it. There was not a thing I could do, so I shut my eyes for an instant. We brought up against a boulder, fortunately, with no special damage - except to my nerves. Not being a man, I don't pretend to having enjoyed that experience - and there, not six feet away, was a ghostly figure that I knew must be Nimrod.

He did not greet me as a long lost, for such I surely felt, but merely remarked in a whisper:

"We are in a cloud cap. It is settling down. The elk are over there. Keep close to me." And he started along the ridge. I felt it was so thoughtful of him to give me this admonition. I would much rather have been returned safely to camp without further injury and before I froze to the saddle; but I grimly kept Blondey's nose overlapping his mate's back and said nothing - not even when I discovered that my cherished riding whip had left me. It probably was not fifty feet away, on that toboggan slide, but it seemed quite hopeless to find anything in the freezing misty grayness that surrounded us.

We continued our perilous passage. Then I was rewarded by a sight seldom accorded to humans. It was worth all the fatigue, cold, and bruises, for that appallingly illogical cloud cap took a new vagary. It split and lifted a little, and there, not three hundred yards away, in the twilight of that cold wet cloud, on that mountain in the sky, were two bull elk in deadly combat. Their far branching horns were locked together, and they swayed now this way, now that, as they wrestled for the supremacy of the herd of does, which doubtless was not far away. We could not see clearly: all was as in a dream. There was not a sound, only the blurred outlines through the blank mist of two mighty creatures struggling for victory. One brief glimpse of this mountain drama; then they sank out of sight, and the numbing grayness and darkness once more closed around us.

On the way back to camp, Blondey shied at a heap of decaying bones that were still attached to a magnificent pair of antlers. They were at the foot of a cliff, over which the animal had probably fallen. The gruesome sight was suggestive of the end of one of those shadowy creatures, fighting back there high up on the mountain in the mist and the darkness.

We saw no mountain sheep, but oh, the joy of our camp fire that night! For we got back in due time all right - Nimrod and the gods know how. To feel the cheery dancing warmth from the pine needles driving away cold and misery was pure bliss. One thing is certain about roughing it for a woman: - there is no compromise. She either sits in the lap of happiness or of misery. The two are side by side, and toss her about a dozen times a day - but happiness never lets her go for long.

VIII.

AT YEDDAR'S.

Life at Yeddar's ranch on Green River, where Nimrod and I left the pack train, is different from life in New York; likewise the people are different. And as every Woman-who-goes-hunting-with-her-husband is sure to go through a Yeddar experience, I offer a few observations by way of enlightenment before telling how I killed my antelope. (If you wish to be proper, always use the possessive for animals you have killed. It is a Western abbreviation in great favour.)

A two-story log house, a one-room log office, a log barn, and, across the creek, the log shack we occupied, fifty miles from the railroad, and no end of miles from anything else, but wilderness - that was Yeddar's.

Old Yeddar - Uncle John, the guides and trappers and teamsters called him - had solved the problem of ideal existence. He ran this rough road house without any personal expenditure of labour or money. He sold whisky in his office to the passing teamsters and guides, and relied upon the same to do the chores around the place, for which he gave them grub, the money for which came from the occasional summer tourist, such as we.

Mrs. Spiker 'did' for him in the summer for her board and that of her little girl, and in the winter he and a pard or two rustled for themselves, on bacon, coffee, and that delectable compound of bread and water known as camp sinkers. He got some money for letting the horses from two Eastern outfits run over the surrounding country and eat up the Wyoming government hay. Thus he loafs on through the years, outside or inside his office, without a care beyond the getting of his whisky and his tobacco. Of course he has a history. He claims to be from a 'high up' Southern family, but has been a plainsman since 1851. He has lived among the Indians, has several red-skinned children somewhere on this planet, and seems to have known all the wild tribe of stage drivers, miners, and frontiersmen with rapid-firing histories.

Once a week, if the weather were fine, Uncle John would tie a towel and a clean shirt to his saddle, throw one leg across the back of Jim, his cow pony, blind in one eye and weighted with years unknown, and the two would jog a mile or so back in the mountains, to a hot sulphur spring, where Yeddar would perform his weekly toilet. He was not known to take off his clothes at any other time, and if the weather were disagreeable the pilgrimage was omitted.

The cheapest thing at Yeddar's, except time, was advice. You could not tie up a dog without the entire establishment of loafers bossing the job. A little active co-operation was not so easy to get, however. One day I watched a freighter get stuck in the mud down the road 'a piece.' One by one, the whole number of freighters, mountaineers and guides then at Yeddar's lounged to the place, until there were nine able-bodied men ranged in a row watching the freighter dig out his wagon. No one offered to help him, but all contented themselves with criticising his methods freely and inquiring after his politics.

During the third week of our stay, Uncle John raised the price of our board - and such board! - giving as an excuse that when we came he did not know that we were going to like it so well, or stay so long! Please place this joke where it belongs.

The charm that held us to this rough place was the abundance of game. The very night we got there, I was standing quietly by the cabin door at dusk, when down the path came two of the prettiest does that the whole of the Blacktail tribe could muster. Shoulder to shoulder, with their big ears alert, they picked their way along, and under cover of the deepening twilight advanced to examine the dwelling of the white man.

I watched them with silent breath. They were not ten yards away. Then they saw me and, wheeling around, stopped, the boldest a little in advance of her companion, with the right forefoot raised for action. I made no move. The graceful things eyed me suspiciously for several seconds and then advanced a little in a one-sided fashion.

A laugh from Yeddar's office, across the creek, where Uncle John and Dave were having a quiet game of pinochle, caused a short retreat up the road. About fifty yards away, they stopped, and there, in the twilight, in that wild glen, they put themselves through a series of poses so graceful, so unstudied, so tender, so deer-like, that my heart was thrilled with joy at the mere artistic beauty of the scene. Then the loudmouthed alarm of a dog sent them silently into the forest gloom.

Nimrod wanted some photographs of animals from life, and the energy which we put forth to obtain these was a constant surprise and disturbance to Uncle John and his co-loafers. They could understand why one might trap an animal, but to let it go again unhurt, after spending hours over it with a camera, was a problem that required many drinks and much quiet cogitation in the shade of the office.

For days we tried to get a wood-chuck. At last we succeeded, and I find this note written in my journal for that date: -

"Oct. 15th: Nimrod caught a woodchuck to-day, a baby one, and we called him Johnny. Johnny stayed with us all day in his cage, while Nimrod made a sketch of him and I took his picture. Then, in the late afternoon, we took him back to his home in the stone-clad hill, and put him among his brothers and sisters, who peeped cautiously at us from various rocky niches, higher up the hill."

Little Johnny must have had a great deal to say of the strange ways and food of the big white animal. It must have been hard, too, for him to have found suitable woodchuck language to express his sensations when he was carried, oh! such a long way, in a big sack that grew on the side of his captor; and of the taste of peppermint candy, which he ate in his prettiest style, sitting on his haunches and clutching the morsel in both forepaws like any well-bred baby woodchuck. And then those delicious sugar cookies that Mrs. Spiker had just baked! How could he make his ignorant brother chuckies appreciate those cookies! Poor little Johnny is a marked woodchuck. He has seen the world.

When Nimrod went hunting skunks, the group at the office gave us up. "Locoed, plumb locoed," was the verdict.

Have you ever been on a skunk hunt? But perhaps you have no prejudices. I had. My code of action for a skunk was, if you see a black and white animal, don't stop to admire its beautiful bushy tail, but give a good imitation of a young woman running for her life. This did not suit Nimrod. He assured me that there was no danger if we treated his skunkship respectfully, and, as I was the photographer, I put on my old clothes and meekly fell in line. Nimrod set several box traps in places where skunks had been. These traps were merely soap boxes raised at one end by a figure four arrangement of sticks, so that when the animal goes inside and touches the bait the sticks fall apart, down comes the box, and the animal is caged unhurt. The next morning we went the rounds. The first trap was unsprung. The second one was down. Of course we could not see inside. Was it empty? Was the occupant a rat or a skunk, and if so, *what* was he going to do?

Nimrod approached the trap. Just then a big tree chanced to get between me and it. I stopped, thinking that as good a place as any to await developments.

"It's a skunk all right," Nimrod announced gleefully.

The box was rather heavy, so Nimrod went to Yeddar's, which was not far away, to see if he could get one of the loungers to help carry the captive to a large wire cage that we had rigged up near our shack.

There were six men near the office, bronzed mountaineers, men of guns and grit, men who had spent their lives facing danger; but, when it came to facing a skunk, each looked at Nimrod as one would at a crazy man and had important business elsewhere. For once I thoroughly appreciated their point of view, but as there was no one else I took one end of the box, and we started. It was a precarious pilgrimage, but we moved gently and managed not to outrage the little animal's feelings.

When the men saw us coming across the creek, with one accord they all went in and took a drink.

We gingerly urged Mr. Skunk into the big cage, and with the greatest caution, never making a sudden move, I took his picture. All was as merry as a marriage bell, and might have continued so but for that puppy Sim. That is the trouble with skunks; they will lose their manners if startled, and *dogs startle skunks*.

Of course the puppy barked; of course the skunk did not like it. He ruffled up his cold black nose, and elevated his bushy tail - his beautiful, plumy tail. I opened the door of his cage and, snatching the puppy, fled. The skunk was a wise and good animal, really a gentleman, if treated politely. He appreciated my efforts on his behalf. He forbearingly lowered his tail, composed his fur, and walked out of the cage and into the near-by woods as tamely as a house tabby out for a stroll.

IX.

MY ANTELOPE.

It was a week later when I did something which those old guides could understand and appreciate - I made a dead shot. I committed a murder, and from that time, the brotherhood of pards was open to us, had we cared to join. It was all because I killed an antelope.

Nimrod and I started out that morning with the understanding that, if we saw antelope, I was to have a chance.

In about six miles, Nimrod spied two white specks moving along the rocky ridge to the east of us, which rose abruptly from the plain where we were. I was soon able to make out that they were antelope. But the antelope had also seen us, and there was as much chance of getting near to them, by direct pursuit, as of a snail catching a hare. So we rode on calmly northward for half a mile, making believe we had not seen them, until we passed out of sight behind a long hill. Then we began an elaborate detour up the mountain, keeping well out of sight, until we judged that the animals, providing they had not moved, were below us, under the rocky ledge nearly a mile back.

We tied up the horses on that dizzy height, and stole,

Nimrod with a carbine, I with the rifle, along a treacherous, shaly bank which ended, twenty feet below, in the steep rocky bluffs that formed the face of the cliff. Every step was an agony of uncertainty as to how far one would slide, and how much loose shale one would dislodge to rattle down over the cliff and startle the antelope we hoped were there. To move about on a squeaking floor without disturbing a light sleeper is child's play compared with our progress. A misstep would have sent us flying over the cliff, but I did not think of that - my only care was not to startle the shy fleet-footed creatures we were pursuing. I hardly dared to breathe; every muscle and nerve was tense with the long suspense.

Suddenly I clutched Nimrod's arm and pointed at an oblong tan coloured bulk fifty yards above us on the mountain.

"Antelope! Lying down!" I whispered in his ear. He nodded and motioned me to go ahead. I crawled nearer, inch by inch, my gaze riveted on that object. It did not move. I grew more elated the nearer it allowed me to approach. It was not so very hard to get at an antelope, after all. I felt astonishingly pleased with my performance. Then - rattle, crash - and a stone went bounding down. What a pity, after all my painful contortions not to do it! I instantly raised the rifle to get a shot before the swift animal went flying away.

But it was strangely quiet. I stole a little nearer - and then turned and went gently back to Nimrod. He was convulsed with silent and unnecessary laughter. My elaborate stalk had been made on - a nice buff stone.

We continued our precarious journey for another

quarter of a mile, when I motioned that I was going to try to get a sight of the antelope, which, according to my notion, were under the rock some hundred feet below, and signed to Nimrod to stay behind.

Surely my guardian angel attended that descent. I slid down a crack in the rock three feet wide, which gave me a purchase on the sides with my elbows and left hand. The right hand grasped the rifle, to my notion an abominably heavy awkward thing. One of these drops was eight feet, another twelve. A slip would probably have cost me my life. Then I crawled along a narrow ledge for about the width of a town-house front, and, making another perilous slide, landed on a ledge so close to the creatures I was hunting that I was as much startled as they.

Away those two beautiful animals bounded, their necks proudly arched and their tiny feet hitting the only safe places with unerring aim. They were far out of range before I thought to get my rifle in position, and my random shot only sent them farther out on the plain, like drifting leaves on autumn wind.

It was impossible to return the way I had come; so I rolled and jumped and generally tumbled to the grassy hill below, and waited for Nimrod to go back along the shaly stretch, and bring down the horses the way they had gone up.

Then we took some lunch from the saddle bags and sat down in the waving, yellow grass of the foot hill with a sweep of miles before us, miles of grassy tableland shimmering in the clear air like cloth of gold in the sun, where cattle grow fat and the wild things still are at home.

During lunch Nimrod tried to convince me that he knew all the time that the antelope I stalked on the mountainside was a stone. Of course wives should believe their husbands. The economy of State and Church would collapse otherwise. However, the appearance of a large band of antelope, a sight now very rare even in the Rockies, caused the profitless discussion to be engulfed in the pursuit of the real thing.

The antelope were two miles away, mere specks of white. We could not tell them from the twinkling plain until they moved. We mounted immediately and went after those antelope - by pretending to go away from them. For three hours, we drew nearer to the quietly browsing animals. We hid behind low hills, and crawled down a water-course, and finally dismounted behind the very mound of prairie on the other side of which they were resting, a happy, peaceful family. There were twenty does, and proudly in their midst moved the king of the harem, a powerful buck with royal horns.

The crowning point of my long day's hunt was before me. That I should have my chance to get one of the finest bucks ever hunted was clear. What should I do, should I hit or miss? Fail! What a thought - never!

Just then a drumming of hoofs which rapidly faded away showed that the wind had betrayed us, and the whole band was off like a flight of arrows.

"Shoot! Shoot!" cried Nimrod, but my gun was already up and levelled on the flying buck - now nearly a hundred yards away.

Grace Gallatin Seton-Thompson

Bang! The deadly thing went forth to do its work. Sliding another cartridge into the chamber, I held ready for another shot.

There was no need. The fleet-footed monarch's reign was over, and already he had gone to his happy hunting ground. The bullet had gone straight to his heart, and he had not suffered. But the does, the twenty beating hearts of his harem! There they were, not one hundred yards away, huddled together with ears erect, tiny feet alert for the next bound - yet waiting for their lord and master, the proud tyrant, so strangely still on the ground. Why did he not come? And those two creatures whose smell they feared - why did he stay so near?

They took a few steps nearer and again waited, eyes and ears and uplifted hoofs asking the question, "Why doesn't he come? Why does he let those dreadful creatures go so close?" Then, as we bent over their fallen hero, they knew he was forever lost to them, and fear sent them speeding out of sight.

X.

A MOUNTAIN DRAMA.

But hunting does not make one wholly a brute, crying, 'Kill, kill!' at every chance. In fact I have no more to confess in that line. Another side to it is shown by an incident that happened about a week later.

We were riding leisurely along, a mile or so from the spot where my antelope had yielded his life to my vanity, when we saw, several miles away in the low hills, two moving flecks of white which might mean antelope.

We watched. The two spots came rapidly nearer, and were clearly antelope. We were soon able to make out that one was being chased by the other; then that they were both bucks, the one in the rear much the heavier and evidently the aggressor. Then from behind a hill came the cause of it all - a bunch of lady antelope, who kept modestly together and to one side, and watched the contest that should decide their master. Surely this unclaimed harem was my doing!

All at once, the two on-coming figures saw us. The first one paused, doubtful which of the two dangers to choose. His foe caught up with him. He wheeled and charged in self-defence, their horns met with a crash, and the smaller was thrown to the ground. He was clearly no match for his opponent.

He sprang to his feet. His only safety was in flight, but where? His strength was nearly gone. He ran a short distance away from us, circling our cavalcade. His foe was nearly up to him again. He stopped an instant with uplifted foot, then turned and made directly for *us*. Three loaded guns hung at our saddles, but no hand went towards them. Not thirty feet away from our motionless horses the buck dropped, exhausted. We could easily have lassoed him. His adversary kept beyond gunshot, not daring to follow him into the power of an enemy all wild things fear; and an eagle who had perched on a rock near by, in hopes of a coming feast, flapped his wings and slowly flew away to search elsewhere for his dinner. The conquering buck walked back to his spoils of war, and soon marshalled them out of sight behind a hill.

The young buck almost at our feet quickly recovered. He was not seriously hurt, only frightened and winded. He rose to his feet and stood for an instant looking directly at us, his head with its growing horns held high in the air, as if to thank us for the protection from a lesser foe he had so boldly asked and so freely received of an all powerful enemy. Then, turning, he lightly sped over the plain in an opposite direction, and the eagle, who had kept us in sight until now, perhaps with a lingering hope, rose swiftly upwards and was lost to sight.

One elk with an eleven-point crown, and one antelope, of the finest ever brought down, is the tax I levied on the wild things. Of the many, many times I have watched them and left them unmolested, and of the lessons they have taught me, under Nimrod's guidance, I have not space to tell, for the real fascination of hunting is not in the killing but in seeing the creature at home amid his glorious surroundings, and feeling the freely rushing blood, the health-giving air, the gleeful sense of joy and life in nature, both within and without.

XI.

WHAT I KNOW ABOUT WAHB OF
THE BIGHORN BASIN.

A fourteen-inch track is big, even for a grizzly. That was the size of Wahb's. The first time I saw it, the hole looked big enough for a baby's bath tub.

We were travelling in Mr. A.'s pack train across the Shoshones from Idaho to Wyoming. It was the first of October, and by then, in that region, winter is shaking hands with you - pleasant hands to be sure, but a bit cool. The night before we had made a picturesque camp on the lee side of a rock cliff which was honeycombed with caves. A blazing camp fire was built at the mouth of one of these and we lounged on the rock ledges inside, thoroughly protected from the wind and cold. A storm was brewing. We could hear the pine trees whistle and shriek as they were lashed about in the forest across the brook. The lurid light of the fire showed us ourselves in distorted shadows. The whole place seemed wild and wicked, like a robber camp, and under its spell one thought things and felt things that would have been impossible in the sun shine, where everything is revealed. It began to snow, but we laughed at that. What did it matter in the shelter of the cave? For the first time in days I was thoroughly toasted on all sides at once. We had changed abruptly from the steam-heated Pullman to camping in snow, and it takes a few days to get used to such a shock. We told tales as weird as the scene, until far into the night. The next morning the sun was bright, but the cook had to cut a hole in the ice blanket over the brook to get water. We dared not linger at our robber camp, for at any time a big snowstorm might come that would cover the Wind River Divide, which we had to cross, with snow too deep for the horses to travel.

Two days later, the weather still promising well, we decided to camp for a few days on the Upper Wiggin's Fork to hunt. It was a lovely spot; one of those little grassy parks which but for the uprising masses of mountains and towering trees might have surrounded your country home.

That first night as we sat around the camp fire there came out of the blackness behind us a faint greeting - *Wheres Who - Wheres Who* - from a denizen of this mountain park, the great horned owl. The next morning we packed biscuits into our saddle-bags and separated for the day into two parties, Nimrod and the Horsewrangler, the Host and myself, leaving the Cook to take care of camp. We were hunting for elk, mountain lion, or bear. Nimrod had his camera, as well as his gun, a combination which the Horsewrangler eyed with scant tolerance.

The Host led me down the Wiggin's Fork for two miles, when we came out upon a sandy, pebbly stretch which in spring the torrents entirely covered, but now had been dried up for months. I was following mechanically, guiding Blondey's feet among the cobblestones, for nature had paved the place very badly, without much thought for anything beyond the pleasure of being alive, when the Host suddenly stopped and pointed to the ground. There I made out the track of a huge bear going the way we were, and beyond was another, and another. Then they disappeared like a row of post-holes into the distance. The Host said there was only one bear in that region that could make a track like that; in spite of the fact that this was beyond his range, it must be Meeteetsee Wahb. He got off his horse and measured the track. Yes, the hind foot tracked fourteen inches. What a hole in the ground it looked!

The Host said the maker of it was probably far away, as he judged the track to be several weeks old. I had heard so many tales of this monster that when I gazed upon his track I felt as though I were looking at the autograph of a hero.

We saw other smaller grizzly and black bear tracks that day, so it was decided to set a bear bait. Our Host was a cattle king, and could wage war on bears with a good conscience. The usual three-cornered affair of logs was fixed, the trap in the centre and elk meat as a decoy. Horse meat is more alluring, but we deemed we would not need that, since we had with us "a never-failing bear charm." Its object was to suggest a lady bear, and thus attract some gallant to her side. The secret of the preparation of this charm had been confided to Nimrod by an old hunter the year before. It was a liquid composed of rancid fish oil, and - but I suppose I must not tell. A more ungodly odour I have never known. Nimrod put a few drops of it on his horse's feet, and all the other horses straightway ostracised him for several days till the worst of it wore away. Even the cook allowed "it was all-fired nasty." So some of this bear charm went on the bait.

The next morning, as we started out for the day to roam the mountains, we first inspected the bear pen. Nothing had been near it. Indeed that charm would keep everything else away, if not the bear himself.

The next day it was the same story, but this really was no argument for or against the charm, because, as I was told, bears in feeding usually make about a two weeks' circuit, and although we had seen many tracks they were all stale, demonstrating in a rough way that if we could linger for a week or two we would be sure to catch some one of the trackers on the return trip.

This we could not do, as the expected snow-storm was now threatening, and we were still two days from the Divide. To be snowed up there would be serious. Before we could get packed up the snow began, falling steadily and quietly as though reserving its forces for later violence. We had been travelling about an hour from where we broke camp, when Nimrod beckoned me to join him where he had halted with the Horsewrangler a little off the line the pack train was following. I rode up quietly, thinking it might be game. But no; Horsewrangler pointed to a little bank where there was a circular opening in the trees. I looked, but did not understand.

"Do you see that dip in the ground there where the snow melts as fast as it drops?"

"Yes."

"Wal, that there's a bear bath."

"A bear's bath!" I exclaimed, suspecting a hoax.

"Yes, a sulphur spring. I reckon this here one belongs to the Big Grizzly."

We examined the place with much interest, but found no fresh tracks, and the snow had covered most of the stale ones, as "of course he ain't got no call for it in winter. Like as not, he's denned up somewheres near, though it's a mite early."

This was thrilling. Perhaps we might pass within a few feet of Wahb and never know it. It was like being told that the ghost of the dear departed is watching you. Nimrod pointed out to me a tree with the bark scratched and torn off for several feet - one of Wahb's rubbing trees. He located the sunning ledge for me, and then we reluctantly hurried on, for the journey ahead promised to be long and hard. Indeed I found it so.

There were many indications that the storm was a serious one, and not the least of these was the behaviour of the little chief hare, or pika. As we ascended the rocky mountain-side we saw many of these little creatures scurrying hither and thither with bundles of hay in their mouths, which they deposited in tiny hay-cocks in sheltered places under rocks. So hard were they working that they could not even stop to be afraid of us. As all the party, but myself, knew, this meant bad weather and winter; for these cute, overgrown rats are reliable barometers, and they gave every indication that they were belated in getting their food supply, which had been garnered in the autumn after the manner of their kind, properly housed for winter use.

All that day we worked our way through the forest with the silent snow deepening around us, ever up and up, eight thousand, nine thousand, ten thousand feet. It was an endless day of freezing in the saddle, and of snow showers in one's face from the overladen branches. I was frightfully cold and miserable. Every minute seemed the last I could endure without screeching. But still our Host pushed on. It was necessary to get near enough to the top of the Continental Divide so that we could cross it the next day. It began to grow dark about three o'clock; the storm increased. I kept saying over and over to myself what I was determined I should not say out loud:

"Oh, please stop and make camp! I cannot stay in this saddle another minute. My left foot is frozen. I know it is, and the saddle cramp is unbearable. I am so hungry, so cold, so exhausted; oh, please stop!" Then, having wailed this out under my breath, I would answer it harshly: "You little fool, stop your whimpering. The others are made of flesh and blood too. We should be snowbound if we stopped here. Don't be a cry-baby. There is lots of good stuff in you yet. This only seems terrible because you are not used to it, so brace up."

Then I would even smile at Nimrod who kept keen watch on me, or wave my hand at the Host, who was in front. This appearance of unconcern helped me for a few seconds, and then I would begin the weary round: "Oh, my foot, my back, my head; I cannot endure it another moment; I can't, I can't." Yet all the while knowing that I could and would. Thus I fought through the afternoon, and at last became just a numb thing on the horse with but one thought, "I can and will do it." So at last when the order came to camp in four feet of snow ten thousand feet above the sea, with the wind and snow blowing a high gale, I just drew rein and sat there on my tired beast.

We disturbed a band of mountain sheep that got over the deep snow with incredible swiftness. It was my first view of these animals, but it aroused no enthusiasm in me, only a vague wonder that they seemed to be enjoying themselves. Finally Nimrod came and pulled me off, I was too stiff and numb to get down myself. Then I found that the snow was so deep I could not go four feet. Not to be able to move about seemed to me the end of all things. I simply dropped in the snow - it was impossible to ever be warm and happy again - and prepared at last to weep.

But I looked around first - Nimrod was coaxing a pack animal through the snow to a comparatively level place where our tent and bed things could be placed. The Host was shovelling a pathway between me and the spot where the Cook was coaxing a fire. The Horse-wrangler was unpacking the horses alone (so that I might have a fire the sooner). They were all grim - doubtless as weary as I - but they were all working for my ultimate comfort, while I was about to repay them by sitting in the snow and weeping. I pictured them in four separate heaps in the snow, all weeping. This was too much; I did not weep. Instead by great effort I managed to get my horse near the fire, and after thawing out a moment unsaddled the tired animal, who galloped off gladly to join his comrades, and thus I became once more a unit in the economic force. But bad luck had crossed its fingers at me that day without doubt, and I had to be taught another lesson. I tell of it briefly as a warning to other women; of course - men always know better, instinctively, as they know how to fight. I presume you will agree that ignorance is punished more cruelly than any other thing, and that in most cases good intentions do not lighten the offence. My ignorance that time was of the effect of eating snow on an empty stomach. My intentions were of the best, for, being thirsty, I ate several handfuls of snow in order to save the cook from getting water out of a brook that was frozen. But my punishment was the same - a severe chill which made me very ill.

I had been cold all day, but that is a very different thing from having a chill. I felt stuffed with snow; snow water ran in my veins, snow covered the earth, the peaks around me. I was mad with snow. They gave me snow whisky and put me beside a snow fire. I had not told any one what I had done, not realising what was the mischief maker, and it really looked as though I had heart disease, or something dreadful.

They put rugs and coats around me till I could not move with their weight; but they were putting them around a snow woman. The only thing I felt was the icy wind, and that went through my shivering, shaking self. The snow was falling quietly and steadily, as it had fallen all day. We *must* cross yonder divide to-morrow. It was no time to be ill. Every one felt that, and big, black gloom was settling over the camp, when I by way of being cheerful remarked to the Host: "Do you-ou kno-ow, I feel as though there was n-nothing of me b-but the sno-ow I ate an hour ago."

"Snow!" he exclaimed. "Did you eat much? Well, no wonder you are ill."

The effect was instantaneous. Everybody looked relieved; I was not even a heroine.

"I will soon cure you," said the Host, as he poured out more whisky, and the Cook reheated some soup and chocolate. The hot drinks soon succeeded in thawing me from a snow woman back to shivering flesh and blood which was supportable.

Nimrod looked pleasant again and began studying the mountain sheep tracks. The cook fell to whistling softly from one side of his mouth, while a cigarette dangled from the other, as was his wont when he puttered about the fire. The Horsewrangler was making everything tight for the night against wind and snow. The Host lighted a cigarette, a calm expression glided over his face, and he became chatty, and, although the storm was just as fierce and the thermometer just as low, peace was restored to Camp Snow.

The next day we crossed the divide, and not a day too soon. The snow was so deep that the trail breaker in front was in danger of going over a precipice or into a rock crevice at any time. After him came the pack, animals, so that they could make a path for us. The path was just the width of the horse, and in some places the walls of it rose above my head. In such places I had to keep my feet high up in the saddle to prevent them from being crushed. For a half day we struggled upwards with danger stalking by our sides, then on the very ridge of the divide itself, 11,500 feet in the air, with the icy wind blowing a hurricane of blinding snow, we skirted along a precipice the edge of which the snow covered so that we could not be sure when a misstep might send us over into whatever is waiting for us in the next world.

But fortunately we did not even lose a horse. Then came the plunging down, down, with no chance to pick steps because of the all-concealing snow. Those, indeed, were "stirring times," but we made camp that night in clear weather and good spirits. We were on the right side of the barrier and only two days from the Palette Ranch - and safety, not to say luxury.

If you had Aladdin's lamp and asked for a shooting box, you could hardly expect to find anything more ideal than the Palette Ranch. There is no spot in the world more beautiful or more health giving. It is tucked away by itself in the heart of the Rockies, 150 miles from the railroad, 40 miles from the stage route, and surrounded on the three sides by a wilderness of mountains. And when after travelling over these for three weeks with compass as guide, one dark, stormy night we stumbled and slipped down a mountain side and across an icy brook to its front lawn, the message of good cheer that streamed in rosy light from its windows seemed like an opiate dream.

We entered a large living room, hung with tapestries and hunting trophies where a perfectly appointed table was set opposite a huge stone fireplace, blazing with logs. Then came a delicious course dinner with rare wines, and served by a French chef. The surprise and delight of it in that wilderness - but the crowning delight was the guestroom. As we entered, it was a wealth of colour in Japanese effect, soft glowing lanterns, polished floors, fur rugs, silk-furnished beds and a crystal mantelpiece (brought from Japan) which reflected the fire-light in a hundred tints. Beyond, through an open door, could be seen the tiled bathroom. It was a room that would be charming anywhere, but in that region a veritable fairy's chamber. Truly it is a canny Host who can thus blend harmoniously the human luxuries of the East and the natural glories of the West.

In our rides around the Palette I saw Wahb's tracks

once again. The Host had taken us to a far away part of his possessions. Three beautiful wolf hounds frisked along beside us, when all at once they became much excited about something they smelt in a little scrub-pine clump on the right. We looked about for some track or sign that would explain their behaviour. I spied a huge bear track.

"Hah!" I thought, "Wahb at last," and my heart went pit-a-pat as I pointed it out to Nimrod. He recognised it but remained far too calm for my fancy. I pointed into the bushes with signs of "Hurrah, it's Wahb." I received in reply a shake of the head and a pitying smile. How was I to know that the dogs were saying as plainly as dogs need to "A bobcat treed"?

So I followed meekly and soon saw the bobcat's eyes glaring at us from the topmost branches. The Host took a shot at it with the camera which the lynx did not seem to mind, and calling off the disappointed dogs we went on our way. The Host allows no shooting within a radius of twelve miles of the Palette. Any living thing can find protection there and the result is that any time you choose to ride forth you can see perfectly wild game in their homeland.

* * * * *

It was not till the next year that I really saw Wahb. It was at his summer haunt, the Fountain Hotel in the Yellowstone National Park. If you were to ask Nimrod to describe the Fountain geyser or Hell Hole, or any of the other tourist sights thereabouts, I am sure he would shake his head and tell you there was nothing but bears around the hotel. For this the occasion when Nimrod spent the entire day in the garbage heap watching the bears, while I did the conventional thing and saw the sights.

About sunset I got back to the hotel. Much to my surprise I could not find Nimrod; and neither had he been seen since morning, when he had started in the direction of the garbage heap in the woods some quarter of a mile back from the hotel. Anxiously I hurried there, but could see no Nimrod. Instead I saw the outline of a Grizzly feeding quietly on the hillside. It was very lonely and gruesome. Under other circumstances I certainly would have departed quickly the way I came, but now I must find Nimrod. It was growing dark, and the bear looked a shocking size, as big as a whale. Dear me, perhaps Nimrod was inside - Jonah style. Just then I heard a sepulchral whisper from the earth.

"Keep quiet, don't move, it's the Big Grizzly."

I looked about for the owner of the whisper and discovered Nimrod not far away in a nest he had made for himself in a pile of rubbish. I edged nearer.

"See, over there in the woods are two black bears. You scared them away. Isn't he a monster?" indicating Wahb.

I responded with appropriate enthusiasm. Then after a respectful silence I ventured to say:

"How long have you been here?"

"All day - and such a day - thirteen bears at one time. It is worth all your geysers rolled into one.

"H'm - Have you had anything to eat?"

"No." Another silence, then I began again.

"Aren't you hungry? Don't you want to come to dinner?"

He nodded yes. Then I sneaked away and came back as soon as possible with a change of clothes. The scene was as I had left it, but duskier. I stood waiting for the next move. The Grizzly made it. He evidently had finished his meal for the night, and now moved majestically off up the hill towards the pine woods. At the edge of these he stood for a moment, Wahb's last appearance, so far as I am concerned, for, as he posed, the fading, light dropped its curtain of darkness between us, and I was able to get Nimrod away.

XII.

THE DEAD HUNT.

To hunt the wily puma, the wary elk, or the fleet-footed antelope is to have experiences strange and varied, but for the largest assortment of thrills in an equal time the 'dead hunt' is the most productive. My acquaintance with a 'dead hunt' - which is by no means a 'still hunt' - began and ended at Raven Agency. It included horses, bicycles, and Indians, and followed none of the customary rules laid down for a hunt, either in progress or result.

And, not to antagonise the reader, I will say now that it was very naughty to do what I did, an impolite and ungenerous thing to do, on a par with the making up of slumming parties to pry into the secrets of the poor. It was the act of a vandal, and at times - in the gray dawn and on the first day of January - I am sorry about it; but then I should not have had that carved bead armlet, and as that is the tail of my story, I will put it in the mouth and properly begin.

Nimrod and I went to the United States agency for the Asrapako or Raven Indians in - well, never mind, not such a far cry from the Rockies, unless you are one of those uncomfortable persons who carry a map of the United States in your mind's eye - because Burfield

Grace Gallatin Seton-Thompson

was there painting Many Whacks, the famous chief; because Nimrod wanted to know what kind of beasties lived in that region; and because I wanted a face to face encounter with the Indian at home. I got it.

The first duty of a stranger at Raven Agency is to visit the famous battlefield, three miles away; and the Agent, an army officer, very charmingly made up a horseback party to escort us there. He put me on a rawboned bay who, he said, was a "great goer." It was no merry jest. I was nearly the last to mount and quite the first to go flying down the road. The Great Goer galloped all the way there. His mouth was as hard as nails, and I could not check him; still, the ride was no worse than being tossed in a blanket for half an hour. On the very spot, I heard the story of the tragic Indian fight by one who claimed to have been an eye-witness. Every place where each member of that heroic band fell, doing his duty, is marked by a small marble monument, and as I looked over the battle ground and saw these symbols of beating hearts, long still in death, clustered in twos and threes and a dozen where each had made the last stand, every pillar seemed to become a shadowy soldier; the whole awful shame of the massacre swept over me, and I was glad to head my horse abruptly for home. And then there were other things to think about, things more intimate and real. No sooner did the Great Goer's nose point in the direction of his stable than he gave a great bound, as though a bee had stung him; then he lowered his head, laid back his ears, and - gallopped home.

I yanked and tugged at the bit. It was as a wisp of hay in his mouth. I might as well have been a monkey or a straw woman bobbing up and down on his back. Pound, pound, thump, thump, gaily sped on the Great

Goer. There were dim shouts far behind me for a while, then no more. The roadside whipped by, two long streaks of green. We whizzed across the railroad track in front of the day express, accompanied by the engine's frantic shriek of "down brakes." If a shoe had caught in the track - ah! I lost my hat, my gold hatpin, every hairpin, and brown locks flew out two feet behind.

Away went my watch, then the all in two pockets, knife, purse, match-box - surely this trail was an improvement on Tom Thumb's' bread crumbs. One foot was out of the stirrup. I wrapped the reins around the pommel and clung on. There is a gopher hole - that means a broken leg for him, a clavicle and a few ribs for me. No; on we go. Ah, that stony brook ahead we soon must cross! Ye gods, so young and so fair! To perish thus, the toy of a raw-boned Great Goer!

Pound, pound, pound, the hard road rang with the thunder of hoofs. Could I endure it longer? Oh, there is the stream - surely he will stop. No! He is going to jump! It's an awful distance! With a frantic effort I got my feet in the stirrups. He gathered himself together. I shut my eyes. Oh! We missed the bank and landed in the water - an awful mess. But the Great Goer scrambled out, with me still on top somehow, and started on. I pulled on the reins again with every muscle, trying to break his pace, or his neck anything that was his. Then there was a flapping noise below. We both heard it, we both knew what it was - the cinch worked loose, that meant the saddle loose.

In desperation I clutched the Great Goer's mane with both hands and, leaning forward, yelled wildly in his ears:

"Whoa, whoa! The saddle's turning! Whoa! Do you wa-ant to *ki-lll* me?"

Do not tell me that the horse is not a noble, intelligent animal with a vast comprehension of human talk and sympathy for human woe. For the Great Goer pulled up so suddenly that I nearly went on without him in the line of the least resistance. Then he stood still and went to nibbling grass as placidly as though he had not been doing racing time for three miles, and I should have gone on forever believing in his wondrous wit had I not turned and realised that he was standing in his own pasture lot.

Seeking to console my dishevelled self as I got off, I murmured, "Well, it was a sensation any way - an absolutely new one," just as Nimrod gallopped up, and seeing I was all right, called out:

"Hello, John Gilpin!" That is the way with men.

My scattered belongings were gathered up by the rest of the party, and each as he arrived with the relic he had gathered, made haste to explain that his horse had no chance with my mount.

I thanked the Agent for the Great Goer without much comment. (See advice to Woman-who-goes-hunting-with-her-husband.) But that is why, the next day, when Burfield confided to me that he knew where there were some 'Dead-trees' (not dead trees) that could be examined without fear of detection, I preferred to borrow the doctor's wife's bicycle.

Dead-trees? Very likely you know what I did not until I saw for myself, that the Asrapako, in common with several Indian tribes, place their dead in trees instead of in the ground. As the trees are very scarce in that arid country, and only to be found in gullies and along the banks of the Little Big Buck River, nearly every tree has its burden of one or more swathed-up bodies bound to its branches, half hidden by the leaves, like great cocoons - most ghastly reminders of the end of all human things.

It was to a cluster of these "deadtrees," five miles away, that Burfield guided me, and it was on this ride that the wily wheel, stripped of all its glamour of shady roads, tête-à-têtes, down grades, and asphalts, appeared as its true, heavy, small seated, stubborn self.

I can undertake to cure any bicycle enthusiast. The receipt is simple and here given away. First, take two months of Rocky Mountains with a living sentient creature to pull you up and down their rock-ribbed sides, to help out with his sagacity when your own fails, and to carry you at a long easy lope over the grassy uplands some eight or ten thousand feet above the sea in that glorious bracing air. Secondly, descend rapidly to the Montana plains - hot, oppressive, enervating - or to the Raven Agency, if you will, and attempt to ride a wheel up the only hill in all that arid stretch of semi desert, a rise of perhaps three hundred feet.

It is enough. You will find that your head is a sea of dizziness, that your lungs have refused to work, that your heart is pounding aloud in agony, and you will then and there pronounce the wheel an instrument of torture, devised for the undoing of woman.

I tried it. It cured me, and, once cured, the charms of

the wheel are as vapid as the defence of a vigilant committee to the man it means to hang. Stubborn - it would not go a step without being pushed. It would not even stand up by itself, and I literally had to push it - it, as well as myself on it - in toil and dust and heat the whole way. Nimrod said his bicycle betrayed itself, too, only not so badly. Of course, that was because he was stronger. The weaker one is, the more stubbornly bicycles behave. Every one knows that. And they are so narrow minded. They needs must stick to the travelled road, and they behave viciously when they get in a rut. Imagine hunting antelope across sagebrush country on a bicycle! I know a surveyor who tried it once. They brought him home with sixteen broken bones and really quite a few pieces of the wheel, improved to Rococo. Bah! Away with it and its limitations, and those of its big brother, the automobile! Sing me no death knell of the horse companion.

At last, with the assistance of trail and muscle, the five miles were covered, and we came to a dip in the earth which some bygone torrent had hollowed out, and so given a chance for a little moisture to be retained to feed the half-dozen cottonwoods and rank grass, that dared to struggle for existence in that baked up sagebrush waste which the government has set aside for the Raven paradise.

We jumped - no, that is horse talk - we sprawled off our wheels and left the stupid things, lying supinely on their sides, like the dead lumpish things they are, and descended a steep bank some ten feet into the gully.

It was a gruesome sight, in the hour before sunset, with not a soul but ourselves for miles around. The lowering sun lighted up the under side of the leaves and branches and their strange burdens, giving an effect uncanny and weird, as though caused by unseen footlights. Not a sound disturbed the oppressive quiet, not the quiver of a twig. Five of the six trees bore oblong bundles, wrapped in comforters and blankets, and bound with buckskin to the branches near the trunk, fifteen or twenty feet from the ground, too high for coyotes, too tight for vultures. But what caught our attention as we dropped into the gully was one of the bundles that had slipped from its fastenings and was hanging by a thong.

It needed but a tug to pull it to the ground. Burfield supplied that tug, and we all got a shock when the wrappings, dislodged by the fall, parted at one end and disclosed the face of a mummy. I had retreated to the other end of the little dip, not caring to witness some awful spectacle of disintegration; but a mummy - no museum-cased specimen, labelled 'hands off', but a real mummy of one's own finding - was worth a few shudders to examine.

I looked into the shrivelled, but otherwise normal, face of the Indian woman. What had been her life, her heart history, now as completely gone as though it had never been - thirty years of life struggle in snow and sun, with, perhaps, a little joy, and then what?

Seven brass rings were on her thumb and a carved wooden armlet encircled the wrist. These I was vandal enough to accept from Burfield. There were more rings and armlets, but enough is enough. As the gew-gaws had a peculiar, gaseous, left-over smell, I wrapped them in my gloves, and surely if trifles determine destiny, that act was one of the trifles that determined

92   Grace Gallatin Seton-Thompson

the fact that I was to be spared to this life for yet a while longer. For, as I was carelessly wrapping up my spoil, with a nose very much turned up, Burfield suddenly started and then began bundling the wrappings around the mummy at great speed. Something was serious. I stooped to help him, and he whispered:

"Thought I heard a noise. If the Indians catch us, there'll be trouble, I'm afraid."

We hastily stood the mummy on end, head down, against the tree, and tried to make it look as though the coyotes had torn it down, after it had fallen within reach, as indeed they had, originally. Then we crawled to the other end of the gully, scrambled up the bank, and emerged unconcernedly.

There was nothing in sight but long stretches of sage brush, touched here and there by the sun's last gleams. We were much relieved. Said Burfield:

"The Indians are mighty ugly over that Spotted Tail fight, and if they had caught us touching their dead, it might have been unhealthy for us."

"Why, what would they do?" I asked, suddenly realising what many white men never do - that Indians are emotional creatures like ourselves. The brass rings became uncomfortably conspicuous in my mind.

"Well, I don't suppose they would dare to kill us so close to the agency, but I don't know; a mad Injun's a bad Injun."

Nevertheless, this opinion did not deter him from

climbing a tree where three bodies lay side by side in a curious fashion; but I had no more interest in 'dead-trees,' and fidgeted. Nimrod had wandered off some distance and was watching a gopher hole-up for the night. The place in the fading light was spooky, but it was of live Indians, not dead ones, that I was thinking.

There is a time for all things, and clearly this was the time to go back to Severin's dollar-a-day Palace Hotel. I started for the bicycles when two black specks appeared on the horizon and grew rapidly larger. They could be nothing but two men on horseback approaching at a furious gallop. It was but yaller-covered-novel justice that they should be Indians.

"Quick, Burfield, get out of that tree on the other side!" It did not take a second for man and tree to be quit of each other, at the imminent risk of broken bones. I started again for the wheels.

"Stay where, you are," said Burfield; "we could never get away on those things. If they are after us, we must bluff it out."

There was no doubt about their being after us. The two galloping figures were pointed straight at us and were soon close enough to show that they were Indians. We stood like posts and awaited them. Thud, thud - ta-thud, thud - on they charged at a furious pace directly at us. They were five hundred feet away - one hundred feet - fifty.

Now, I always take proper pride in my self possession, and to show how calm I was, I got out my camera, and as the two warriors came chasing up to the fifty-foot limit, I snapped it. I had taken a landscape a minute

Grace Gallatin Seton-Thompson

before, and I do not think that the fact that that landscape and those Indians appeared on the same plate is any proof that I was in the least upset by the red men's onset. Forty feet, thirty - on they came - ten - were they going to run us down?

Five feet, full in front of us they pulled in their horses to a dead stop - unpleasantly, close, unpleasantly sudden. Then there was an electric silence, such as comes between the lightning's flash and the thunder's crack. The Indians glared at us. We stared at the Indians, each measuring the other. Not a sound broke the stillness of that desolate spot, save the noisy panting of the horses as they stood, still braced from the shock of the sudden stop.

For three interminable minutes we faced each other without a move. Then one of the Indians slowly roved his eyes all over the place, searching suspiciously. From where he stood the tell-tale mummy was hidden by the bank and some bushes, and the tell-tale brass rings and armlet were in my gloves which I held as jauntily as possible. He saw nothing wrong. He turned again to us. We betrayed no signs of agitation. Then he spoke grimly, with a deep scowl on his ugly face:

"No touch 'em; savey?" giving a significant jerk of the head towards the trees.

We responded by a negative shake of the head. Oh, those brass rings! Why did I want to steal brass rings from the left thumb of an Indian woman mummy! Me! I should be carving my name on roadside trees next!

There was another silence as before. None of us had changed positions, so much as a leaf's thickness. Then the second Indian, grim and ugly as the first, spoke sullenly:

"No touch 'em; savey?" He laid his hand suggestively on something in his belt.

Again we shook our heads in a way that deprecated the very idea of such a thing. They gave another dissatisfied look around, and slowly turned their horses.

We waited breathless to see which way they would go. If they went on the other side of the gully, they must surely see that bundle on the ground and - who can tell what might happen? But they did not. With many a look backwards, they slowly rode away, and with them the passive elements of a tragedy.

I tied my ill-gotten, ill-smelling pelt on the handle bar of the doctor's wife's bicycle, and we hurried home like spanked children. That night, after I had delivered unto the doctor's wife her own, and disinfected the gewgaws in carbolic, I added two more subjects to my Never-again list - bicycling in Montana and 'dead hunts.'

XIII.

JUST RATTLESNAKES.

It is a blessing that a rattlesnake has to coil before it can spring. No one has ever written up life from a rattler's point of view, although it has been unfeelingly stated that fear of snakes is an inheritance from our simian ancestors.

To me, I acknowledge, a rattler is just a horrid snake; so, when we were told at Markham that rattlers were more common than the cattle which grazed on every hill, I discovered that there were yet new imps to conquer in my world of fear. Shakspere has said some nice things about fear - "Of all the wonders, ... it seems to me most strange that men should fear" - but he never knew anything about squirming rattlesnakes.

The Cuttle Fish ranch is five miles from Markham. That thriving metropolis has ten houses and eleven saloons, in spite of Dakota being 'prohibition.' Markham is in the heart of the Bad Lands, the wonderful freakish Bad Lands, where great herds of cattle range over all the possible, and some of the impossible, places, while the rest of it - black, green, and red peaks, hills of powdered coal, wicked land cuts that no plumb can fathom, treacherous clay crust over boiling lava, arid horrid miles of impish whimsical Nature - is

Bad indeed.

Nimrod and I had been lured to the Cuttle Fish ranch to go on a wolf hunt. The house was a large two storey affair of logs, with a long tail of one storey log outbuildings like a train of box cars. We sat down to dinner the first night with twenty others, a queer lot truly to find in that wild uncivilised place. There was an ex-mayor and his wife from a large Eastern city; a United States Senator - the toughest of the party - who appeared at table in his undershirt; four cowboys, who were better mannered than the two New York millionaires' sons who had been sent there to spend their college vacation and get toughened (the process was obviously succeeding); they made Nimrod apologise for keeping his coat on during dinner; the three brothers who owned the ranch, and the wife of one of them; several children; a prim and proper spinster from Washington - how she got there, who can tell? - and Miss Belle Hadley, the servant girl.

In studying the case of Belle I at last appreciated the age-old teaching that the greatest dignity belongs to the one who serves. Else why did the ex-mayor's wife bake doughnuts, and the rotund Senator toil at the ice cream freezer with the thermometer at 112 degrees, and the millionaires' sons call Belle "Miss Hadley," and I make bows for her organdie dress, while she curled her hair for a dance to be held that evening ten miles away, and to which she went complacently with her pick of the cowboys and her employers' two best horses, while they stayed at home and did her work! Else why did this one fetch wood for her, that one peel the potatoes, another wash the dishes? And when she and the rest of us were seated at meals, and something was needed from the kitchen, why did the unlucky one nearest the door jump up and forage? Belle was never nearest the door. She sat at the middle of the long table, so that she could be handy to everything that was 'circulating.' But I refer this case to the author of those delightful papers on the "Unquiet Sex," and hark back to my story.

That night the moon was full, and the coyotes made savage music around the lonely ranch house. First from the hill across the creek came a snappy *wow-wow, yac-yac*, and then a long drawn out *ooo-oo*; then another voice, a soprano, joined in, followed by a baritone, and then the star voice of them all - loud, clear, vicious, mournful. For an instant I saw him silhouetted against the rising moon on the hill ridge, head thrown back and muzzle raised, as he gave to the peaceful night his long, howling bark, his "talk at moon" as the Indians put it. The ranchman remarked that there were "two or three out there," but I knew better. There were dozens, perhaps hundreds, of them; I am not deaf.

The next morning we were up with the dawn and started by eight to run down Mountain Billy, the grey wolf who lived on the ranchmen of the Bad Lands. Our outfit was as symmetrical as a pine cone; - dogs, horses, mess wagon, food, guns and men. All we needed was the grey wolf. I was the only woman in the party, and, like "Weary Waddles," tagged behind.

It was the middle of September, and the weather should have known better. But it was the Bad Lands, and there was a hot spell on. By three o'clock the thermometer showed 116-1/2 in the shade, and I believed it. The heat and glare simmered around us like fire. The dogs' tongues nearly trailed in the baked dust, the horses' heads hung low, an iron band seemed ever tightening around my head, as the sun beat down upon all alike with pitiless force.

When we came to the Little Missoula, even its brackish muddy water was welcome, and I shut my eyes to the dirt in the uninviting brown fluid, and my mind to the knowledge of the horrid things it would do to me, and drank; Tepid, gritty, foul - was it water I had swallowed? The horse assigned to me, a small, white, benevolent animal named 'Whiskers,' waded in knee deep and did the same. Whiskers was a 'lady's horse,' which, being interpreted, meant aged eighteen or twenty, with all spirit knocked out by hard work; a broken down cow pony, in fact, or, in local parlance, a 'skate,' a 'goat.' He had lagged considerably behind the rest of the party.

However, Whiskers did not matter; nothing mattered but the waves on waves of heat that quivered before my eyes. I shut them and began repeating cooling rhymes, such as 'twin peaks snow clad,' 'From Greenland's Icy Mountains,' and the 'Frozen North,' by way of living up to Professor James' teachings. Whiskers was ambling on, half-stupefied with the heat, as I was, when from the road just in front came a peculiar sound. I did not know what it was, but Whiskers did, and he immediately executed a demi volte (see Webster) with an energy I had not thought him capable of.

Again came the noise, yes, surely, just as it had been described - like dried peas in a pod - and gliding across the road was a big rattlesnake. I confess had Whiskers been so inclined, I should have been content to have passed on with haughty disdain. But Whiskers performed a left flank movement so nearly unseating me that I deemed it expedient to drop to the ground, and Whiskers, without waiting for orders, retreated down the road at what he meant for a gallop. The rattler stopped his pretty gliding motion away from me, and seemed in doubt. Then he began to take on a few quirks. "He is going to coil and then to strike," said I, recalling a paragraph from my school reader. It was an unhappy moment! I knew that tradition had fixed the proper weapons to be used against rattlesnakes: a stone (more if necessary), a stick (forked one preferred), and in rare cases a revolver (when it is that kind of a story). I had no revolver. There was not a stick in sight, and not a stone bigger than a hazelnut; but there was the rattler. I cast another despairing glance around and saw, almost at my feet and half hidden by sage brush, several inches of rusty iron - blessed be the passing teamster who had thrown it there. I darted towards it and, despite tradition, turned on the rattler armed with the goodly remains of - a frying pan.

The horrid thing was ready for me with darting tongue and flattened head - another instant it would have sprung. *Smash* on its head went my valiant frying pan and struck a deadly blow, although the thing managed to get from under it. I recaptured my weapon and again it descended upon the reptile's head, settling it this time. Feeling safe, I now took hold of the handle to finish it more quickly. Oh, that tail - that awful, writhing, lashing tail! I can stand Indians, bears, wolves, anything but that tail, and a rattler is all tail, except its head. If that tail touches me I shall let go. It did touch me, I did not let go. Pride held me there, for I heard the sound of galloping hoofs. Whiskers' empty saddle had alarmed the rest of the party.

My snake was dead now, so I put one foot on him to take his scalp - his rattles, I mean - when horrid thrills coursed through me. The uncanny thing began to wriggle and rattle with old-time vigour. I do not like to think of that simian inheritance. But, fortified by Nimrod's assurance that it was 'purely reflex neuro-ganglionic movement,' I hardened my heart and captured his 'pod of dry peas.'

Oh, about the wolf hunt! That was all, just heat and rattlesnakes.

The hounds could not run; one died from sunstroke while chasing a jack rabbit. No one lifted a finger if it could be avoided. All the world was an oven, and after three days we gave up the chase, and leaving Mountain Billy panting triumphantly somewhere in his lair, trailed back to the ranch house with drooping heads and fifteen rattle-snakes' tails. Oh, no, the hunt was not a failure - for Mountain Billy.

XIV.

AS COWGIRL.

Till the time of the "WB" round-up all cows looked alike to me. We were still at the Cuttle Fish ranch, which was in a state of great activity because of the fall roundup. Belle, the servant girl, had received less attention of late and had been worked harder, a combination of disagreeables which caused her to threaten imminent departure. The cowboys, who had been away for several days gathering in the stragglers that had wandered into the wild recesses of those uncanny Bad Land hills, assembled in full force for the evening meal, and announced, between mouthfuls, that the morrow was to be branding day for the several outfits, about two thousand head of cattle in all, the 'WB' included, which were rounded up on the Big Flat two miles distant from the ranch.

This was the chance for me to be relieved of my crass ignorance concerning round-ups, really to have a definite conception of the term instead of the sea of vagueness and conjecture into which I was plunged by the usual description - "Oh, just a whole lot of cattle driven to one place, and those that need it are cut out and frescoed." How many was a whole lot, how were they driven, where were they driven from, what were they cut out with, how were they branded, and when did they need it? My ignorance was hopeless and pathetic, and those to whom I applied were all too familiar with the process to be able to describe it. I might as well have asked for a full description of how a man ate his dinner.

"Will you take me to the round-up to-morrow?" I asked of the 'WB' boss.

"Well, I could have a team hitched up, and Bob could drive you to the Black Nob Hill, where you can get a good view," was the tolerant reply.

Bob had wrenched his foot the day before, when roping a steer, and was therefore incapacitated for anything but 'woman's work' - 'a soft job.'

"Oh, but I do not want to be so far away and look on; I want to be *in* it."

He looked at me out of the angle of his eye to make sure that I was in earnest. "Tain't safe," he said.

"Then you mean to say that every cowboy risks his life in a round-up?"

"Oh, well, they're men and take their chances. Besides, it's their business."

I never yet have been able to have a direct question answered by a true mountaineer or plainsman by a simple yes or no. Is there something in the bigness of their surroundings that causes the mind to spread over an idea and lose directness like a meadow brook?

However, by various wiles known to my kind, the next

morning at daybreak I was mounted upon the surest-footed animal in the 'bunch.'

"She's a trained cow pony and won't lose her head," the boss remarked.

Thus equipped, I was allowed to accompany the cowboys to their work, with the understanding that I was to keep at a safe distance from the herd. Van Anden, a famous 'cutter out,' whatever that meant, was deputed to have an especially watchful eye upon me. Van Anden was a surprisingly graceful fellow, who got his six foot of stature in more places during the day than any of the smaller men. He was evidently a cowboy because he wanted to be one. There were many traces of a college education and a thorough drilling in good manners in an Eastern home, which report said could still be his if he so wished; and report also stated that he remained a bachelor in spite of being the most popular man in the country, because of a certain faithless siren who with gay unconcern casts languishing glances and spends papa's dollars at Newport.

But this was no Beau Brummel day. There was work to do, and hard work, as I soon discovered. We had ridden perhaps a mile; my teeth were still chattering in the early morning cold (breaking ice on one's bath water and blowing on one's fingers to enable one to lace heavy boots may suit a cowboy: I do not pretend to like it), when we began to notice a loud bellowing in the distance. Instantly my companions spurred their horses and we went speeding over the Little Missoula bottom lands, around scrub willows and under low hanging branches of oak, one of which captured my hat, after breaking both of the hat pins, and nearly swept me from the saddle.

On I rushed with the rest, hatless, and as in a cloud of fury. Van Anden took a turn around that tree and was at my side again with the hat before I realised what, he was doing. I jerked out a "thank you" between lopes, and of course forbore to remark that a hat without pins was hollow mockery. I dodged the next low branch so successfully that the pommel in some miraculous way jumped up and smashed the crystal in my watch, the same being carried in that mysterious place, the shirt waist front, where most women carry their watches, pocket books, and love letters.

When we got into the open the terrible bellowing - a combination of shriek, groan, and roar in varying pitch - grew louder, and I could just discern a waving ghostly mass in the gray morning mist. I wondered if this were the herd, but found it was only the cloud of dust in which it was enveloped.

Four of the cowboys had already disappeared in different directions. I heard the 'WB' boss say, "Billy, to the left flank. Van, them blamed heifers," as he flew past them.

Van dashed forward, I gave my black mare a cut with the quirt and followed. Van's face, as he turned around to remonstrate, was a study of surprise, distress, and disgust, for I was undoubtedly breaking rules.

"Don't bother about me," I called as airily as possible, as I shot past him. He had checked his horse's speed, but now there was nothing to do but to follow me as fast as he could. I shall have to record that he swore, as he turned sharply to the right into a group of cattle.

Grace Gallatin Seton-Thompson

Poor man, it was dreadful to saddle him with a woman at such a juncture, but I was not a woman just then. I was a green cowboy and frightened to death, as the cattle closed around me, a heavy mass of ponderous forms, here wedged in tightly and bellowing, some with the pain of being crushed, some for their calves. I expected every instant to be trampled under foot.

"Stick to your horse, whatever you do, and work to the left," I heard Van shouting to me over the backs of a dozen cows. The dust, the noise, and the smell of those struggling creatures appalled and sickened me. How was I ever going to work to the left in that jam? I could see nothing but backs and heads and horns. I allowed myself one terrified groan which was fortunately lost in the general uproar. But the pony had been in such a situation before, if I had not, and she taught me what to do. She gave a sudden spring forward when a space just big enough for her appeared, then wove her way a few paces forward between two animals who had room enough on the other side of them to give way a little, while the space I had just left had closed up, a tight mass of groaning creatures.

Thus we worked our way to the left whenever there was a chance, and at last through the dust I could see the heavenly open space beyond. Forgetting my tactics, I made straight for it, and was caught in one of those terrible waves of tightly pressed creatures which is caused by those on the outside pressing towards the centre, and the centre giving until there is no more space, when comes the crush. Fortunately I was on the outskirts of this crush, and by holding my feet up high we managed to squeeze through that dreadful, dust covered, stamping, snorting bedlam into the glorious free air and sunshine. Already I had a much better conception of what a 'whole lot' of cattle meant.

From the vantage ground of a little hill I could see the whole herd, and realised that I had been in only a small bunch of it, composed of cows and calves. Had I gone to the right I should soon have gotten into a raging mass of some thousand head of bulls. They were pawing and tearing up the ground that but a little before had been covered with grass and late flowers, and occasionally goring one another. The cowboys were riding on the outskirts of this life-destroying horde, forcing the stragglers back into line, and by many a sudden dash forward, then to the right, sharp wheel about, and more spurts this way and that, were slowly driving it toward another mass of cattle, a half mile further on, which could be distinguished only by the clouds of dust which enveloped it.

Van Anden, meanwhile, in the small bunch with which I had had such an intimate acquaintance, was acting as though he had lost his wits, or so it seemed to me until I began to understand what he was doing. He would dart into the bunch, scattering cattle right and left, and would weave in and out, out and in, waving his arms, shouting, throwing his rope, occasionally hitting an animal across the nose or the flank, sometimes twisting their tails, dodging blows and kicks, and finally emerge driving before him a cow followed by her calf. These another cowboy would take charge of and drive to a small bunch of cows and calves which I now noticed for the first time, separating them from their relations, who remonstrated in loud bellowings, stampings and freakish, brief, ill judged attacks. And then I understood what it meant to 'cut out' cattle from 'a whole lot.'

When the calves and cows were finally separated, it was necessary to drive them also to the Big Flat for the afternoon's work of branding those that 'needed it.' Van guarded the rear of the bunch and of course I rode with him, that is as near as I could, for he was as restless as a blue bottle fly in a glass jar, dashing hither and thither, keeping those crazy creatures together, and ever pushing them forward. The dust and heat and noise and smell and continual action made my head ache. So this was cowboy life, Van's choice! I thought of a certain far away, well ordered home, with perhaps a sweet voiced mother and well groomed sister, and wondered, even while I knew the answer. On the one hand, peace, comfort, affection, and the eternal sameness; on the other, effort, hardship, fighting sometimes, but ever with the new day a whole world of unlived possibilities, change, action, and bondage to no one.

A particularly fractious heifer at this point suddenly changed my contemplation of Van Anden's character into a lively share of Van Anden's job. The creature was making good time straight towards me, and as I had dropped considerably behind the herd in order to breathe some fresh air and to be free from the dust, I knew that it meant a long hard chase for Van and his tired horse if I did not head off that heifer; I felt I owed him that much. I had seen the cowboys do that very thing a hundred times that morning, but you cannot stand on your toe by watching a ballet dancer do it. However, I started on a gallop, slanting diagonally towards the creature, swinging one arm frantically (I really could not let go with both) and yelling "Hi, hi!" I wondered what would happen next, for to be honest, I was exquisitely scared. Why scared? It is not for me to explain a woman's dread of the unknown and untried.

I heard Van shouting, but could not understand. To know you are right and then go ahead is a pretty plan, but how to know? The animal did not stop or swerve from its course. We would surely collide. What was I to do? Oh, for a precedent! Evidently the mare was aware of one, for she wheeled to the right just in time to miss the oncoming heifer, and we raced alongside for a few seconds. I had so nearly parted company with my mount in the last manoeuvre (centaurs would have an enormous advantage as cowboys) that I had lost all desire to help Van and only wanted to get away from that heifer, to make an honourable dismount, and go somewhere by myself where a little brook babbled nothings, and the forget-me-nots placidly slept. Rough riding and adventures of the Calamity Jane order tempted me no more.

Whether now the heifer did the proper thing or not, I cannot say, but she circled around with me on the outer side (I suspect my cow pony knew how it was done) and was half way back to the herd when Van took it in charge. His face bore a broad grin for the first time that day, from what emotions caused I have never been able to determine. I, of course, said nothing.

Then, oh, the joy of that round up dinner! The 'WB' outfit had a meal tent, a mess wagon, and a cook for the men, and a rope corral, food and water for the horses. Everybody was happy for the noon hour, save the unlucky ones whose turn it was to guard the herd. Bob had driven the ex-mayor's wife, the sad eyed spinster, and Nimrod over to join us at dinner. The boss greeted Nimrod with the assurance that I was 'all right' and could apply any time for a job. I may as well say that Nimrod had allowed me to go without him in the morning, because the cattle business was no novelty to him; because daybreak rising did not appeal to him as a pastime; and because, at the time I broached the subject, being engaged in writing a story, he had removed but one-eighth of his mind for the consideration of mundane affairs, and that, as any one knows, is insufficient to judge fairly whether the winged thing I was reaching out for was a fly or a bumble bee. In the morning, the story being finished and the other seven-eights of brain at liberty to dwell upon the same question, he decided to follow me, with the result that in the afternoon I rode in the wagon.

The cowboy meal, which I believe was not elaborated for us, was a healthy solid affair of meat, vegetables, hot biscuit, coffee, and prunes, appetisingly cooked and unstintingly served, for the Bad Land appetite is like unto that of the Rocky Mountains, lusty and big. The saddling of fresh horses made a lively scene for a few moments in the corral; then the men rode off for the afternoon's business of branding.

The ranch party packed itself into a three-seated buckboard and we followed behind. We went at a wide safe distance from the half-crazed herds, which had been driven this way and that until they knew not what they wanted, nor what was wanted of them, to where a huge fire was blazing and rapidly turning cold black iron to red hot. These irons were fashioned in curious shapes, from six to ten inches long and fastened to a four foot iron handle. The smell of burning flesh was in the air, and horrid shrieks. Beyond was the ceaseless bellowing and stamping and weaving of the herds.

From the time I got into the wagon and became a mere onlooker, my point of view changed. The exhilaration of action had disappeared. I was a cowboy no longer.

The cattle in the morning had been stupid foolish creatures, dangerous in their blind strength, which must be made to do what one willed. Now they were poor, dumb, persecuted beasts which must be tormented, even tortured (for who shall say that red hot iron on tender flesh is not torture?) and eventually butchered for the swelling of man's purse. I saw the riders dash towards an animal who 'needed branding' - which I discovered to mean one that had hitherto escaped the iron, or that had changed owners - throw a rope over its head or horns, fasten the other end to the pommel, and drag it to the fire, where it was thrown and tied. Then it was seized by several men who sat on its head and legs to hold it comparatively still while another took the hot brand from the fire and pressed it against the quivering side of the animal. It was then released and, bawling with pain and fright, allowed to return to its mother, who had been kept off by another rider. A sound at my side informed me that the little old maid was weeping copiously.

It is a pity I could not have had the cowboy's point of view, for mine was most unpleasant, but my little glimpse of the other side was gone, and gladly I drove away from the mighty smells and sounds of that unfortunate mass of seething life, subjected to the will of a dozen men, Van Anden the worst of the lot. And as we went silently through the sweet cool air, crisp as an October leaf, where a bluebird was twittering a wing-free song on the poplar yonder, where silver-turned willows were gently swaying, and a jolly chipmunk was rippling from log to stone, I wondered whether the Newport girl had really done so wrong after all.

XV.

THE SWEET PEA LADY SOMEONE ELSE'S MOUNTAIN SHEEP.

It was at Winnipeg (you do not want to know how we got there) that I first walked into the aura of the Sweet Pea Lady, and by so doing prepared the way for the shatterment of another illusion - namely, that 'little deeds of kindness' always result in mutual pleasure.

Flowers and fruit in Manitoba are treasured as sunshine in London, for you must remember that Manitoba is a very new country, that it is only a paltry few thousands of years since its thousands of miles were scraped flat as a floor. Everything even yet looks so immodest on those vast stretches. The clumps of trees stand out in such a bold brazen fashion. The houses appear as though stuck on to the landscape. Even an honest brown cow can not manage to melt herself into the endless stretch of prairies. In fact, the little scenic accidents of trees and hollows, which mean fruit and flowers, are mainly due to man.

So, when our friends who saw us off on the west-bound Canadian Pacific left in our sleeper two huge bouquets of sweet peas and ten pounds of blackberries, we knew that the finest garden in Winnipeg had been rifled to do us pleasure. Now, I dearly love flowers and fruit, as I did the giver, but ten pounds of great, fat blackberries and an armful of sweet peas in a cramped stuffy Pullman caused my heart to resound in the minor chords. We rallied again and again to demolish the fruit as we voyaged, and sat with one foot on top of the other to avoid crushing the lovely pea blossoms as we fidgeted about, but the results of our efforts, messy fruit in hopeless abundance and withering leaves in dreary profusion, were discouraging.

When the noon hour came, Nimrod carried the fruit basket into the Diner and set it down on the table. The waiter eyed us askance. "It's a dollar each for dinner, sah." It was clear we were emigrants. We paid the waiter's demand and then from soup to coffee ate blackberries - blackberries until we were black in the mouth and pale in the face. Then we picked up our basket, upon the contents of which our labours had apparently made no impression, and, hastily pushing a plate over the rich red stain it had left on the table cloth, departed with our fruit and a grieved feeling in the region of our hearts. It may not be amiss to remark that I have never eaten a blackberry since. To get to our car it was necessary to pass through another sleeper, where I noticed a made up berth in which was reclining a young woman, and hovering over her solicitously a man, evidently the husband.

Hope and joy awoke within me - perhaps she would like some blackberries! No, she would not venture to eat fruit, and with many thanks, oh, many, many thanks, she declined it. But the blessedness of giving I felt must be mine, so I bribed the porter to take as many sweet peas as he could carry and present them to the sick lady in the next car, and on no account to tell where he got them. I did not want the thanks, neither did I want the sweet peas, but I was illogical enough to hope that the Recording Angel would be busy and accept the act at its face value as a "deed of kindness."

It must have been a slack day with the angel, for this is a brief but accurate account of what followed, and I am willing to leave it to any human, whether my punishment was not out of all proportion to the offense committed:

One hour later. Train stops for ten minutes. I got out for fresh air and promenade on platform. Behold, the first object that meets my gaze is the sick lady, miraculously recovered. She swooped down upon me with the deadly light of determination in her eyes. I was discovered. There was no escape. I was going to be thanked - and I was thanked. Up and down, backwards and forwards, inside and out, and all hands around. And when she paused breathless her husband took up the theme. It seems she was a semi invalid, and the sweet peas were quite the most heavenly thing that could have happened to her. Nimrod joined me at this moment and he was thanked separately and dually, for being the husband of his wife, I suppose. At last we were able to retire with profuse bows, tired but exceedingly thankful that the incident, though trying, was ended.

Three minutes later. Have been driven indoors by the sweet pea woman, as each turn of the walk brought us face to face, when it immediately became necessary to nod and smile, and for our husbands to lift hats and smile, until we looked like loose-necked manikins. At least, the sleeper is tranquil, if stuffy.

Supper time. Have been thanked again by the Sweet

Pea Lady, who sat at our table. She had sweet peas in her hair, and at her belt. The husband had a boutonnière of them.

Next morning, Carberry. Bade an elaborate farewell to the Sweet Pea Lady. She is going straight to the coast where they catch steamer for Japan. Praise be to Allah! I shall see her no more. The heavy polite is wearing.

Next day, Banff Hot Springs. First person on the hotel steps I see is the S.P. Lady. She rushed up and assured me that the S.P.'s were still fresh, and that she and her husband had unexpectedly stopped over for a day.

Next day. Spent the day avoiding S.P.L. Left for Glacier House in the evening. At least, I shall not see S.P.L. there, as they have to go right through to catch steamer.

Two days later, Glacier House. Had horrid shock. Found apparition of S.P. Lady sitting beside me at breakfast table. She began to speak, then I knew it was the real thing. She assured me that many of the S.P.'s were still fresh, as she had clipped their stems night and morning. I again said good by to her, and to those ghastly flowers. She just has time to catch her steamer.

Three days later: Vancouver. Ran across the S.P. Lady in hotel corridor. She saw me first. There was another weary interchange of the heavy polite. Her steamer had been delayed from sailing for two days - in order that we might meet again, I have no doubt.

Next morning. She's gone. Ring the bells, boom the cannon! I saw the Japan steamer bear the Sweet Pea Lady rapidly into deep water. At last easeful peace may again dream on my shoulder. When I returned to the hotel the clerk handed me an envelope enclosing a lady's visiting card (kind fate, she lives in Japan) on which was written "In grateful appreciation of your kindness," and with the card were two sprays of Pressed Sweet Peas.

After this when it comes to "scattering deeds of kindness on the weary way," I shall be the woman who didn't, and who shall say me nay? However, all this flower and fruit piece was but an episode; the event of that journey was the intimate acquaintance we made of the Great Glacier of the Selkirks, and the nice opportunity I had to lose my life. And the only reason this tale is not more tragic is because, given the choice, I preferred to lose the opportunity rather than the life.

I wonder if I can give any idea to one who has not seen it what a snow slide really is; how it sweeps away every vestige of trees, grass, and roots, and leaves a surface of shirting, unstable earth almost as treacherous as quicksand.

Nimrod and I had paid a superficial visit to the Glacier the day before: that is, we had gone as far as its forefoot, a hard but thoroughly safe climb, and had explored with awe the green glass ice caves with which the Great Glacier has seen fit to decorate its lower line, wonderful rooms of ice, emerald in the shadows, with glacial streams for floors.

So the next morning we started out, intending a little bit to further explore the vast, cold, heartless ice sheet (vaster than all the Swiss glaciers together), but more to hunt for the warm beating heart of a mountain sheep, whose home is here. We had been travelling for miles in the wildest kind of earth upheavals, for the Selkirks are still hard and fast in the grip of the ice king; huge boulders, uprooted trees, mighty mountains, released but recently from the glacial wet blanket, when Nimrod discovered the stale track of a mountain sheep. We followed it eagerly till it brought us across the path of a snow slide. At that point it was about five hundred feet across, at an angle of forty-five degrees; below us a thousand feet was a vicious looking glacial torrent; above, an equal distance, was the lower edge of the glacier, the mother of all this devastation.

The fearless-footed mountain sheep had crossed this sliding crumbling earth and gravel incline with apparent ease. For us it was go on or go back. There was no middle course. The row of tiny hoof marks running straight across from one safe bank to the other deceived us. It could not be so very difficult. We dismounted; Nimrod threw the bridle over his horse's head and started across, leading his beast. The animal snorted as he felt the foot-hold giving way beneath him, but Nimrod pulled him along. It was impossible to stand still. It would have been as easy for quicksilver to remain at the top of an incline. Amid rattling stones and sliding earth they landed on the firm bank beyond, fully three hundred feet below me.

It was a shivery sight, but I started expecting the horse would follow. He, however, jerked back snorting and trembling, which unexpected move upset my equilibrium, uncertain at best, and I fell. Nothing but the happy chance of a tight grip on the reins kept me from sliding down that dreadful bank, over the rock into the water, and so into eternity (Please pardon the Salvation Army metaphor).

I had barely time to right myself and get out of the way of my horse, which now plunged forward upon the sliding rock with me. The terrified animal lost his head completely. I could not keep away from his hoofs. He would not let me keep in front, I dare not get above for fear I should slip under his feet, or below him for fear he should slide upon me. I lost my balance again while dodging away from him as he plunged and balked, but managed to grab his mane and we both slid a horrible distance. I could hear Nimrod shouting on the bank, but did not seem to understand him. I had the stage, centre front, and it was all I could attend to.

We were now opposite to Nimrod, but only half way across. Such an ominous rolling and tumbling of stones and tons of earth sliding down over the low precipice into the water! I expected to be with it each instant. Nimrod had started out after me.

Then I understood what he was shouting: "Let go that horse." Why, of course! Why had I not thought of that? I did let go and, thus freed, managed to get across, falling, slipping, but still making progress until I reached the safe ground one hundred feet lower in a decidedly dilapidated condition. My animal followed me instinctively for a short distance, and Nimrod got him the rest of the way - I do not know how. It did not interest me then.

And the saddest of all, the mountain sheep had vanished into the unknown, taking his little tracks with him, so we had to go back in a roundabout way, without sheep, without joy - and without a tragedy.

XVI.

IN WHICH THE TENDERFOOT
LEARNS A NEW TRICK.

For those who have driven four-in-hand, this will have no message. But as four-in-hand literature seems to be somewhat limited and my first lesson was somewhat drastic, I shall venture to tell you how it felt.

Of coaching there are two kinds: Eastern coaching, with well-groomed full-fed horses, who are never worked harder than is good for them; with silver-plated harness, and coach with the latest springs and running gear, umbrella rack, horn, lunch larder, and what not; with footmen or postilions, according to the degree of style, to run to the horses' heads at the first hitch; with the gentleman driver in cream box coat and beribboned whip; with everything down to the pole pin correct and immaculate.

Then there is Western coaching, which is more properly termed staging, for which is used any vehicle that will hold together and whose wheels will turn round. This is pulled by half-broken shaggy horses which would kick any man who ventured near them with brush or currycomb, and which are sometimes made to travel until they drop in the road. The harness on such coaching trips is an assortment of single, double, leaders and wheelers sets, mended with buckskin or wire and thrown on irrespective of fit. Lucky the cayuse who happens to be the right size for his harness.

And the driver! No cream box coat for him - provident the one who owns a slicker and a coat of weather green (the same being the result of sun and rain on any given color). And the people in the stage hoist no white and red silk parasols. They are there because they are "going somewhere." My multi-murderous cook taught me the distinction between "just travellin'" and "going somewhere."

As for the roads - oh, those Rocky Mountain roads! They make coaching quite a different thing from that on the smooth boulevards around New York. I have twice made seventy-five miles in twelve hours, by having four relays, but the average rate of travel is about twenty miles in eight hours. And the day when I first took the ribbons in my hands to guide - four horses we were from nine in the morning till five at night going twelve miles. This was the way of it: Nimrod and I were on a hunting trip in the Canadian Rockies, and as the government map said there was a road, though not a good one, we decided to carry our belongings in a four-horse wagon, in which we could also ride if we liked, and to have saddle horses besides.

Green, a man of the region, was the driver and cook, and we had as guest a famous bear hunter from the Sierra Nevadas. On the first two days out from the little mountain town where we started, we saw many tracks of black bear, which encouraged the hunters to think that they might find a grizzly (which, by the way, they did not).

The dust was thick and red, enveloping us all day long like some horrible insistent monster that had resolved itself into atoms to choke, blind and strangle us. Nimrod looked like a clay man - hair, eyebrows, mustache, skin, and clothes were all one solid coating of red dust. We were all alike. Even the sugar, paper-wrapped in the bottom of a box, covered by other boxes, bags and a canvas, became adulterated almost past use.

On the fourth day this changed, and we camped at the foot of a granite mountain. It made one think of the Glass Mountain of fable, with its smooth stretches of polished rock shining in the sun. That a human being should dare to take a wagon over such a place seemed incredible. Yet there the road was, zigzagging up the rocky slope, while here and there the jagged outlines of blasted rock showed where the all-powerful dynamite had been used to make a resting place for straining horses.

That morning excitement surrounded our out-of-door breakfast table. We had had strange visitors during the night, while we slept. A mountain lion, the beautiful tan-coated vibrant-tailed puma, had nosed within ten feet of me and then, not liking the camp-fire glow and unalarmed by my inert form, had silently retreated.

It made me feel creepy to see how easily that lithe-limbed powerful creature might have had me for a midnight meal. But I was not trying to do him harm, and so he granted me the same tolerance. Then, too, not far away was a bear track, and the canned peaches were fewer than the night before.

All of this caused Nimrod and the bear-hunter to

Grace Gallatin Seton-Thompson

saddle their horses early; and agreeing to meet us at night on the other side of the mountain, where the map showed a stream, they set out for a day's hunt. Nimrod's horse having gone slightly lame, I offered mine, a swift-footed intelligent dear, and agreed to ride in the wagon.

It was the same old story. Virtue is somebody else's reward. I never had a worse day in the mountains. Green and I started blithely enough by nine, which had meant a 5:30 rising in the cold gray dawn. The horses had been worked every day since the start, and were jaded.

We went slowly along the only level road in our journey that day; but the load did not seem to be riding well, and at the beginning of the ascent Green got out to investigate. He said the spring was out of order. The wagon was what is known as a thorough-brace, which means that there are two large loopy steel bands on which the wagon box rests; the loops are filled in with countless strips of leather, forming a pad for the springs to play on. (The Century Dictionary will please not copy this definition.) The Deadwood stage coach was a thorough-brace, I believe. Another interesting out-of-date detail in the construction of this wagon was that the brake had no mechanical device for holding it in position when it was put on hard, and the driver had to rely upon his strength of limb to keep it in place. It seems that Green, in pounding these bits of leather in the spring, had badly crushed his left hand. He said nothing to me, and I did not notice that, contrary to custom, he was driving with his right hand, which he usually reserved for the whip and the brake.

We crossed the shallow brook and started up the very

steep and very rocky road, when everything happened at once. Two of the horses refused to pull and danced up and down in the one spot, a sickening thing for a horse to do. This meant the instant application of the brake. We had already begun to slip backward (the most uncomfortable sensation I know, barring actual pain). Nimrod's horse, tied on behind, gave a frightened snort and broke his rope. Green attempted to take the reins with his left hand. They dropped from his grasp, and I saw that his fingers were purple and black.

"Grab the lines, can you?" he said, as he seized the whip and put both feet on the brake. The leaders were curveting back on the wheelers in a way which meant imminent mix up, their legs over traces and behind whiffle-trees. On the right, of us was solid rock up, on the left solid rock down, one hundred feet to the stream, and just ahead was the sharp turn the road made to a higher ledge in its zigzag up the mountain. I had always intended to learn to drive four-in-hand, but this first lesson left me no pleasure in the learning. There were no little triumphs of difficulties mastered, no gentle surprises, no long, smooth, broad, and level stretches with plenty of room to pull a rein and see what would happen. I had to spring into the situation with knowledge, as Minerva did into life, full grown. It was no kindergarten way of learning to drive four-in-hand.

I grabbed the reins in both hands. There were yards of them, rods of them, miles of them - they belonged to a six or sixteen horse set. I do not know which. I sat on them. They writhed in my lap, wrapped around my feet, and around the gun against my knee, in a hopeless and dangerous muddle. Of course the reins were

Grace Gallatin Seton-Thompson

twisted. I did not know one from the other. I gave a desperate jerk which sent the leaders plunging to the right, where fortunately they brought up against the rock wall. Had they gone the other way nothing but our destiny could have saved us from going over the edge. *Crack* went the whip in the right place.

"Slack the lines!" Green cried, as he eased the brake. A lash of the whip for each wheeler, and we started forward, the horses disentangling themselves from the harness as by a miracle, just as the rear wheels were hovering over the bluff. Green dropped the whip (his left hand was quite useless) and straightened out the reins for me.

"Can you do it?" he asked, grasping the whip, as the horses showed signs of stopping again. To attend to the brake was physically impossible. Green could not do it and drive with one hand.

"Yes," I said, "but watch me" - an injunction scarcely necessary.

If ever a woman put her whole mind to a thing, I did on that four-in-hand. There was no place for mistakes. There was no place for anything but the right thing, and do it I must or run the risk of breaking my very dusty, very brown, but none the less precious neck.

A sharp turn in a steep road with rocks a foot high disputing the right of way with the wheels, a heavy load, horses that do not want to pull, and a green driver - that was the situation. If it does not appeal to you as one of the horribles in life, try it once.

"Run your leaders farther up the bank - left, left! *Get*

up, Milo! Frank, get out of that! Now sharp to the right. *Whoa! Steady*! Left - left, I say! *Milo, whoa!* Now to the right, quick! Let 'em on the bank more. *Nellie, easy - Whoa! Steady, George!*" Crack went the whip on the leaders.

"Hold your lines tighter. Pull that nigh leader. *Get out of that, Frank! Now steady, boys*! Don't pull - there!"

Down went the brake; we were safely round the turn, and all hands rested for a moment.

Thus we worked all that morning, Green with the brake, the whip, and his tongue; I with the lines, what strength I had and mother wit in lieu of experience.

There were stretches of two hundred feet of granite, smooth and polished as a floor, where the horses repeatedly slipped and fell, and where the wheels brought forth hollow mocking rumbles.

There were sections where the rocky ledges succeeded one another in steps, and the animals had to pull the heavy wagon up rises from a foot to eighteen inches high by sheer strength - as easy to drive up a flight of brownstone steps on Fifth Avenue. There were places between huge boulders where a swerve of a foot to the right or to the left would have sent us crashing into the unyielding granite.

When we got to the top there was no place to rest - only rock, rock everywhere. No water, no food for the exhausted horses, nothing to do but to push on to the bottom - and such going! Have you ever felt the shuddering of a wagon with brake hard on, as it poised in air the instant before it dropped a foot or two to the next level, from hard rock to hard rock? Have you ever tried to keep four horses away from under a wagon, and yet sufficiently near it not to precipitate the crash? Have you ever at the same time tried to keep them from falling on the rocks ahead and from plunging over the bank as you turn a sharp curve on a steep down grade? If you have, then you know the nature of my first lesson in four-in-hand driving.

We got to the bottom at dusk. I was too tired to speak. Every muscle set up a separate complaint and I had had nothing to eat since morning, as we had expected to make camp by noon. The world seemed indeed a very drab place. We found the hunters careering around searching for us. They thought they had missed us - as they had done the bear.

I have driven, and been driven, hundreds of miles since, but there never was a ride like those twelve, cruel, mocking, pitiless miles over Granite Mountain, when necessity taught me a very pretty trick, which, however, I have not yet been tempted to display at the Madison Square Garden in November.

XVII.

OUR MINE.

It now behooves me to state that, between the events of the last chapter and this, Nimrod and I heard the hum, the wail, and the shriek that make the song of the Westinghouse brake before we found ourselves deposited at the flourishing mining camp of Red Ridge in the Arizona Rockies, nine thousand feet in the air.

Did ever a tenderfoot escape from the mountains without at least having a try at making his or her fortune in a mine - gold one preferred? We, of course, had the chance of our lives, and who knows what might have happened if only the fat woman and the lean woman had not gotten jealous of each other, and thereby wrecked the company?

The gold is, or is not, in the fastnesses of the earth as before, but where, oh, where, is the lean woman of lineage and the fat woman of money? The lean woman had quality. She was the daughter of somebody who had done something, but, unlike *Becky Sharp*, she had not been successful in living richly in San Francisco on nothing a year. Nobody knows whose daughter the fat woman was, but in her very comfortable home in Kansas that had not mattered, and, besides, she had saved a few hundreds.

These two women had husbands, who had entered into a mining scheme together. The man from Frisco was a good-looking, well-educated, jovial fellow, with the purses of several rich friends to back him up, and with a great desire to replenish his purse with the yellow metal direct, rather than to acquire it by the sweat of his brow. He was many other things, but, to be brief, he was a promoter. The man from Kansas had the pride of the uneducated, and a little money, and was also not averse to getting rich fast.

Nimrod, the third partner, likewise encumbered with a wife on the spot, desired to make *his* everlasting fortune, retire from the painting of pictures and the making of books, and grub in the field of science and live happily ever after.

For two weeks we were all together at the only hotel at Cartersville, a hamlet of perhaps thirty souls. It took only two weeks to wreck the company. The mine was a mile and a half away, over a very up-and-down mountain road which on the first day the fat woman and I walked with our husbands, and which Mrs. Frisco and her husband had travelled in Mrs. Kansas' phaeton - the result of a little way Mrs. Frisco had of getting the best.

Three days of this calm appropriation of her carriage while she walked ruffled Mrs. Kansas' temper. When she heard a rumour that Mrs. Frisco had stated disdainfully to the landlady that there could be no thought of recognising Mrs. Kansas socially, but that she must be tolerated because of her money in the enterprise, her politeness grew frigid and the trouble began to brew.

While perfectly willing to watch the logomachy when it should arrive, I had no wish to take part. I was willing to make money, but not to make enemies, so Nimrod and I removed ourselves as much as possible from the Cartersville Hotel, took long walks and rides over the glorious Chihuahua Mountains, poked around the abandoned mines, spied out the deer and mountain lion and the ubiquitous coyote and all the indigenous beasts and birds of the air thereof. We usually managed to arrive at the mine when the partners and their wives were elsewhere.

The mine, *our* mine, was a long horizontal hole in the mountain, with a tiny leaf-choked stream trickling past the entrance, heavy timbers propping up the inert mass of dirt and stone just above our heads, piles of uninteresting rock dumped to one side, the "pay dirt." I had seen such things before, and they had said nothing to me. But this was *our* mine, *our* stream, *our* dump.

McCaffrey, the foreman, put rubber boots on me in the little smithy which formed a part of the entrance of the tunnel, and thus equipped I entered the tunnel. The day shift, represented by two dancing lights far off in the blackness, was preparing to blast.

I advanced uncertainly, my own candle blinding me. Water trickled from the roof and walls of this rock-bound passage seven feet high and four feet wide. A stream of it flowed by the tiny tram track. The hollow sound of the mallet on the crowbar forcing its way into the stubborn wall grew louder as we approached, until we stood with the miners in a foot or so of water which showed yellow and shining in the flickering light of four candles. Then we went back to the smithy to wait the result of the blast.

There was a horrid jarring booming sound. The miners listened intently. McCaffrey said, "One." Another explosion in the tunnel followed - "Two." Another - "Three." Then a silence. "That's bad," said McCaffrey, shaking his head. "An unexploded cap."

"What do you mean?" I asked.

"There were four charges and should have been four explosions. It's liable to go off when we go in there."

"Oh!" I said.

The miners waited a while for the fumes of the dynamite to be dissipated and kept me away from the tunnel mouth, saying:

"If you ever get a dynamite headache you will never want to come near the mine again. And, besides, that unexploded cap may do damage yet."

I went back to the smithy to wait, for it was the last of October, and snow in the mountains at ten thousand feet is cold. I attempted to sit down on a keg behind the little sheet-iron stove, which was nearly red hot.

"You better not sit down on that kaig," said one of the men calmly, without pausing in his work.

"Why?"

"Well, it's dirty, and, besides, it's nitro-glycerine."

"Nitro-glycerine! Why is it in *here*, and so close to the stove? Won't it explode?" and I checked a desire to retreat in disorder.

"No, 't'ain't no danger, if it don't get too hot and ain't jarred. You see, it won't go off if it's too cold, so we keep a little in here and kind o' watch it."

The keg was within two feet of the stove. Suppose that a dog or something were to knock it over! But miners do not suppose.

Just then a tremendous explosion in the tunnel seemed to make the whole earth vibrate. It was followed by a rattling and crashing of rocks, which told us that the last cap had gone off and had done good work.

Half an hour later, when it was safe from dynamite fumes, I went back to our hole in the ground. Nimrod had left me, lured away by some fox tracks trailing up the mountain. The weird scene was too interesting for me to leave until the arrival of the fat and lean women (Mrs. Frisco had persuaded Mrs. Kansas to drive her over) caused me to remember that the parlour fire at the Cartersville Hotel must be very comfortable, and that it was a mile and a half of tiresome snow away.

Evidently the wives of my husband's partners had disagreed on the way, for the air was electric as they greeted me, and to avoid another tête-à-tête they at once turned to accompany me out of the tunnel. I was the last.

The scene was now properly set for a mining accident, so there was nothing for a self respecting tunnel to do but to accordingly, which it did. Just as the fat woman and the lean woman passed into the open air, and I was nearly at the mouth of the tunnel, it caused its roof to cave in so close behind me that, had I not instinctively rushed out, some of the flying stones, timbers, and dirt must have knocked me to the ground.

As it was, I landed sprawling in the snow outside, sweeping the lean woman down with me. It was very like a dime novel. Three lone women who, for purposes of intensification, may be called enemies, staring with white faces at a wall of dirt, and trying to realise that a minute before it had been a black hole. And at the other end of that hole now were two men horribly imprisoned in a rock-walled tomb without air or food, perhaps dead. We could not tell how much of a cave-in it was.

The lean woman rushed for Mrs. Kansas' horse and wagon and went to alarm the hamlet. I dashed up the hill a quarter of a mile to awaken the night shift, who were in their cabin sleeping. And the fat woman at a safe distance wrung her hands and uttered exclamations of horror and ill judged advice to our departing forms.

Between the fright, the altitude, and the hill I had no breath left to speak with as I pounded on the door of the miner's hut. Mountaineers sleep lightly and do not make toilets, so it was barely ten minutes from the time of the cave-in when three men were working at the tunnel's mouth with pickaxes and shovels.

The tunnel had not meant to be malicious, but merely to do the proper thing (it had not even disturbed the nitro-glycerine in the smithy). Not much earth had fallen, and in less than an hour we heard the shouts of the imprisoned men; in two hours they crawled into the air unhurt, and soon were helping the others to shore up the treacherous entrance, so that such a stirring thing could not happen again.

There is not much more to tell. I believe that the tunnel is still there, boring its way into the heart of the mountain, where, perhaps, the lovely yellow gold is; but we no longer refer to it as *ours*, and Nimrod still has to work for our daily jam. For the insolence of Mrs. Frisco in leaving Mrs. Kansas stranded in the snow and obliging her to walk home on the cave-in day developed the brewing storm into such proportions that the next day their husbands did not speak as we gathered round the morning coffee. And the Kansases moved away into one of the other five houses in Cartersville. Mr. Kansas was not "going to see his wife insulted by an upstart - not he: he'd soon show them," and he did so effectively that the Red Ridge Mining Company was soon no more. We docketed our golden dreams 'unusable,' stowed them away, and returned with tranquil minds, if lighter purse, to milder and slower ways of getting rich.

Grace Gallatin Seton-Thompson

XVIII.

THE LAST WORD.

Now this is the end. It is three years since I first became a woman-who-goes-hunting-with-her-husband. I have lived on jerked deer and alkali water, and bathed in dark-eyed pools, nestling among vast pines where none but the four footed had been before. I have been sung asleep a hundred times by the coyotes' evening lullaby, have felt the spell of their wild nightly cry, long and mournful, coming just as the darkness has fully come, lasting but a few seconds, and then heard no more till the night gives place to the fresh sheet of dawn. I have pored in the morning over the big round footprints of a mountain lion where he had sneaked in hours of darkness, past my saddle pillowed head. I have hunted much, and killed a little, the wary, the beautiful, the fleet-footed big game. I have driven a four-in-hand over corduroy roads and ridden horseback over the pathless vasty wilds of the continent's backbone.

I have been nearly frozen eleven thousand feet in air in blinding snow, I have baked on the Dakota plains with the thermometer at 116 degrees, and I have met characters as diverse as the climate. I know what it means to be a miner and a cowboy, and have risked my life when need be, *but*, best of all, I have felt the charm of the glorious freedom, the quick rushing blood, the bounding motion, of the wild life, the joy of the living and of the doing, of the mountain and the plain; I have learned to know and feel some, at least, of the secrets of the Wild Ones. In short, though I am still a woman and may be tender, I am a Woman Tenderfoot no longer.

Choose from Thousands of 1stWorldLibrary Classics By

Adolphus WilliamWard
Aesop
Agatha Christie
Alexander Aaronsohn
Alexander Kielland
Alexandre Dumas
Alfred Gatty
Alfred Ollivant
Alice Duer Miller
Alice Turner Curtis
Alice Dunbar
Ambrose Bierce
Amelia E. Barr
Andrew Lang
Andrew McFarland Davis
Anna Sewell
Annie Besant
Annie Hamilton Donnell
Annie Payson Call
Anton Chekhov
Arnold Bennett
Arthur Conan Doyle
Arthur Ransome
Atticus
B. M. Bower
Basil King
Bayard Taylor
Ben Macomber
Booth Tarkington
Bram Stoker
C. Collodi
C. E. Orr
C. M. Ingleby
Carolyn Wells
Catherine Parr Traill
Charles A. Eastman
Charles Dickens
Charles Dudley Warner
Charles Farrar Browne
Charles Ives
Charles Kingsley
Charles Lathrop Pack
Charles Whibley
Charles Willing Beale
Charlotte M. Braeme
Charlotte M.Yonge
Clair W. Hayes
Clarence Day Jr.
Clarence E. Mulford

Clemence Housman
Confucius
Cornelis DeWitt Wilcox
Cyril Burleigh
D. H. Lawrence
Daniel Defoe
David Garnett
Don Carlos Janes
Donald Keyhole
Dorothy Kilner
Dougan Clark
E. Nesbit
E.P.Roe
E. Phillips Oppenheim
Edgar Allan Poe
Edgar Rice Burroughs
Edith Wharton
Edward J. O'Biren
John Cournos
Edwin L. Arnold
Eleanor Atkins
Elizabeth Cleghorn
Gaskell
Elizabeth Von Arnim
Ellem Key
Emily Dickinson
Erasmus W. Jones
Ernie Howard Pie
Ethel Turner
Ethel Watts Mumford
Eugenie Foa
Eugene Wood
Evelyn Everett-Green
Everard Cotes
F. J. Cross
Federick Austin Ogg
Ferdinand Ossendowski
Francis Bacon
Francis Darwin
Frances Hodgson Burnett
Frank Gee Patchin
Frank Harris
Frank Jewett Mather
Frank L. Packard
Frederick Trevor Hill
Frederick Winslow Taylor
Friedrich Kerst
Friedrich Nietzsche
Fyodor Dostoyevsky

Gabrielle E. Jackson
Garrett P. Serviss
Gaston Leroux
George Ade
Geroge Bernard Shaw
George Ebers
George Eliot
George MacDonald
George Orwell
George Tucker
George W. Cable
George Wharton James
Gertrude Atherton
Grace E. King
Grant Allen
Guillermo A. Sherwell
Gulielma Zollinger
Gustav Flaubert
H. A. Cody
H. B. Irving
H. G. Wells
H. H. Munro
H. Irving Hancock
H. Rider Haggard
H. W. C. Davis
Hamilton Wright Mabie
Hans Christian Andersen
Harold Avery
Harold McGrath
Harriet Beecher Stowe
Harry Houidini
Helent Hunt Jackson
Helen Nicolay
Hendy David Thoreau
Henrik Ibsen
Henry Adams
Henry Ford
Henry Frost
Henry James
Henry Jones Ford
Henry Seton Merriman
Henry Wadsworth
Longfellow
Henry W Longfellow
Herbert A. Giles
Herbert N. Casson
Herman Hesse
Homer
Honore De Balzac

Horace Walpole
Horatio Alger, Jr.
Howard Pyle
Howard R. Garis
Hugh Lofting
Hugh Walpole
Humphry Ward
Ian Maclaren
Israel Abrahams
J.G.Austin
J. Henri Fabre
J. M. Barrie
J. Macdonald Oxley
J. S. Knowles
J. Storer Clouston
Jack London
Jacob Abbott
James Allen
James Lane Allen
James Andrews
James Baldwin
James DeMille
James Joyce
James Oliver Curwood
James Oppenheim
James Otis
Jane Austen
Jens Peter Jacobsen
Jerome K. Jerome
John Burroughs
John F. Kennedy
John Gay
John Glasworthy
John Habberton
John Joy Bell
John Milton
John Philip Sousa
Jonathan Swift
Joseph Carey
Joseph Conrad
Joseph Jacobs
Julian Hawthrone
Julies Vernes
Justin Huntly McCarthy
Kakuzo Okakura
Kenneth Grahame
Kate Langley Bosher
L. A. Abbot
L. T. Meade
L. Frank Baum
Laura Lee Hope

Laurence Housman
Leo Tolstoy
Leonid Andreyev
Lewis Carroll
Lilian Bell
Lloyd Osbourne
Louis Tracy
Louisa May Alcott
Lucy Fitch Perkins
Lucy Maud Montgomery
Lydia Miller Middleton
Lyndon Orr
M. H. Adams
Margaret E. Sangster
Margaret Vandercook
Maria Edgeworth
Maria Thompson Daviess
Mariano Azuela
Marion Polk Angellotti
Mark Overton
Mark Twain
Mary Austin
Mary Cole
Mary Rowlandson
Mary Wollstonecraft Shelley
Max Beerbohm
Myra Kelly
Nathaniel Hawthrone
O. F. Walton
Oscar Wilde
Owen Johnson
P.G.Wodehouse
Paul and Mable Thorn
Paul G. Tomlinson
Paul Severing
Peter B. Kyne
Plato
R. Derby Holmes
R. L. Stevenson
Rabindranath Tagore
Rahul Alvares
Ralph Waldo Emmerson
Rene Descartes
Rex E. Beach
Richard Harding Davis
Richard Jefferies
Robert Barr
Robert Frost
Robert Gordon Anderson
Robert L. Drake

Robert Lansing
Robert Michael Ballantyne
Robert W. Chambers
Rosa Nouchette Carey
Ross Kay
Rudyard Kipling
Samuel B. Allison
Samuel Hopkins Adams
Sarah Bernhardt
Selma Lagerlof
Sherwood Anderson
Sigmund Freud
Standish O'Grady
Stanley Weyman
Stella Benson
Stephen Crane
Stewart Edward White
Stijn Streuvels
Swami Abhedananda
Swami Parmananda
T. S. Ackland
The Princess Der Ling
Thomas A. Janvier
Thomas A Kempis
Thomas Anderton
Thomas Bailey Aldrich
Thomas Bulfinch
Thomas De Quincey
Thomas H. Huxley
Thomas Hardy
Thomas More
Thornton W. Burgess
U. S. Grant
Valentine Williams
Victor Appleton
Virginia Woolf
Walter Scott
Washington Irving
Wilbur Lawton
Wilkie Collins
Willa Cather
Willard F. Baker
William Makepeace Thackeray
William W. Walter
Winston Churchill
Yei Theodora Ozaki
Young E. Allison
Zane Grey